THE ILLUSTRATED LONDON NEWS,

SOCIAL HISTORY
OF VICTORIAN BRITAIN

SOCIAL HISTORY
OF VICTORIAN BRITAIN

BY CHRISTOPHER HIBBERT

ANGUS & ROBERTSON · PUBLISHERS

ANGUS & ROBERTSON · PUBLISHERS
London · Sydney · Melbourne · Singapore · Manila

This edition published by Angus & Robertson (U.K.) Ltd 1975
in conjunction with Sphere Books Ltd
Illustrations copyright © *The Illustrated London News* 1975
Text copyright © Christopher Hibbert 1974

Edited for *The Illustrated London News* by Anthony Gould
Picture research by Reg Smith
Designed by Rod Josey Associates

ISBN 0 207 95657 x

Set in Monotype Baskerville 169

Printed and bound in Great Britain by
Morrison & Gibb Ltd, London and Edinburgh

Contents

Source of Illustrations

The illustrations in this book are, in the main, reproduced from contemporary issues of *The Illustrated London News*. The remainder are from sister papers such as *The Graphic*, *The Sketch* and *The Illustrated Sporting and Dramatic News* which began publication in the second half of the Queen's reign, but which have now ceased publication and form part of the archives of *The Illustrated London News*.

The engravings were originally printed from hand-engraved wood blocks. The box tree provided an exceptionally fine-grained wood with a smooth, hard surface. A second advantage was its toughness. A block could withstand 300,000 impressions from the sustained pounding of steam-driven printing machines. Towards the end of the century the wood block was gradually superseded by the metal half-tone block. The early printed results from these plates were described by G. A. Sala as 'these sooty, smoky and blurred processes', but within a few years improved photographic materials, and the use of glossy paper on which to print the image, resulted in greatly improved quality and far greater speed in the presentation of 'hot' news pictures.

The Illustrated London News picture library now contains one of the world's most comprehensive collections of illustrative material covering practically every aspect of life from 1842 to the present day. During the years of Queen Victoria's reign that are the subject of this book more than a million illustrations were published by *The Illustrated London News*.

Foreword by Sir Arthur Bryant, C.H.

When I was a boy I used to lie on the floor of my father's library turning over the pages of the huge Victorian bound-volumes of *The Illustrated London News*. Beginning in 1842, the fifth year of Queen Victoria's reign, they continued into that of my own lifetime at the turn of the century. Little did I guess that for a period equal to two thirds of that long Victorian era, I, in a later and more troubled century, should be a regular contributor to the same stately historic publication – as much a national institution as *The Times* or the Pavilion at Lord's – and so become, in a humble way, a human part of that long procession in contemporary time-recording.

The wonderful week-by-week record of the past contained in the pictures and letter-press of the Victorian volumes of *The Illustrated London News* spans an epoch of both human progress and human crisis unparalleled by any comparable one in the annals of mankind, except that of the sixty years which followed. The magazine's launching and instantaneous success in 1842 proved almost as remarkable a phenomenon in the population scale of Victorian England, when the politically-conscious proportion of the nation was only a fraction of what it is today, as the universal resort in our own time to television. Within decades of its birth the magazine's circulation exceeded a quarter of a million, and its influence was felt all over the world. In the year 1842, in which Herbert Ingram, the Boston and Nottingham printer – that characteristic early-Victorian embodiment of energy and enterprise – launched this famous and revolutionary (in the best and creative sense of the word) magazine, there occurred the first great clash between the new industrial proletariat and their gradgrind capitalist employers, when the young Tennyson, seeing the angry glow from the factory lights of the starving North and Midland heaths, wrote warningly, of

> 'a hungry people as a lion, creeping nigher,
>   Glares at one that nods and winks behind a slowly dying fire.'

It was the transformation effected by the new railways – another revolution depicted in the early pages of *The Illustrated London News* – which enabled Peel's Government, by the use of its Army, a generation before the Paris Commune of 1871, to contain and defeat without bloodshed a general proletarian rising of the industrial districts. In the same month in which the first issue of *The Illustrated London News* appeared came the dramatic publication of the 'First Report of the Children's Employment Commission', revealing the appalling conditions in which children of seven or eight, and in some cases, three and four, worked in the coalmines – 'harnessed like dogs in a go-cart' – far removed from the pity and conscience of the rulers of a Christian nation. Succeeding volumes record and preserve for posterity the Chartist demonstrations of 1848 and the Great Exhibition of 1851 and, in the same year, the formation of the first national, as distinct from local, trade union, the Amalgamated Society of Engineers. There followed the Crimean and Franco-Prussian Wars and the American Civil War, the unification of Italy and Germany, and the foundation of the International Red Cross and the immense reforms in nursing, hospital administration and hygiene pioneered by Florence Nightingale. In the second half of Victoria's reign came the extensions of the franchise – the 'leap in the dark' of *Punch's* famous cartoon – of 1867 and 1884; the statutory provision of free elementary education, and the beginnings of rate-subsidised housing and social legislation; the liberation of the Balkans from Turkish rule, and the coming-of-age of the self-governing British ocean-nations. All this was accompanied by the industrialisation and urbanisation, on a scale hitherto unimagined, of a formerly mainly rural and pastoral island, the doubling of its population, and the development, inter alia, of electricity and the internal combustion engine.

For the student of history, as Christopher Hibbert's pages show, these giant Victorian tomes, packed with contemporary pictures and accompanying letter-press, constitute the most valuable of any single continuous record of the nation's past over a given period of time. Their detailed presentation of events still far exceeds in accuracy and balance anything which the television cameras and their attendant commentators have yet succeeded in making.

Introduction: 'The World's First Illustrated Weekly Newspaper'

At the beginning of 1842, Herbert Ingram, a young printer from Nottingham, arrived in London. He brought with him the recipe for 'a marvellous pill' which he had purchased some time before in partnership with his brother-in-law, Nathaniel Cooke. This pill, so the partners claimed, had been regularly taken by Thomas Parr, the celebrated Shropshire countryman, whose extraordinary feat of begetting a bastard child at the age of one hundred and five, and living thereafter for a further forty-seven years was attributable to its beneficial qualities. It had sold extremely well in Nottingham as a panacea for all manner of ills from diarrhoea to constipation, as a tonic that gave 'fresh vigour to the whole body' and 'increased the beauty of women'. And Ingram hoped that his fortune would be made if, by advertising the pill more widely, he could make it as popular in London as it was in his home town.

As a printer and newsagent as well as the proprietor of 'Old Parr's Life Pills', Ingram had another and more ambitious idea. He had noticed how the demand for the *Weekly Chronicle* always increased whenever it contained a woodcut as an illustration. This was not very often, for newspapers usually concentrated on reporting the news at length rather than illustrating it, and the appearance of an accompanying picture – such as that of the House of Commons in *The Sunday Times* after the fire of 1834 – was not a common sight. So Ingram had decided to bring out a paper which would contain pictures every week. At first he had thought of making it a record of crime, since this was a subject which always found eager readers. But after approaching Henry Vizetelly to help him in his endeavour, he was persuaded to change his mind. Vizetelly, a wood-engraver whose fanciful portrait of 'Old Parr' was used in advertisements of the pills and on the labels of the bottles in which they were sold, agreed that the idea of a weekly illustrated paper was a good one. But he suggested that it would be better not to concentrate exclusively on crime: a paper of a more general character would enjoy a wider success.

Convinced that Vizetelly was right, Ingram began to make more detailed plans. He rented a publishing office; he recruited artists and journalists; he employed as editor an improvident though skilful writer, Frederick William Naylor Bayley, known as 'Omnibus' Bayley after the name of a publication he more or less single-handedly produced. And on 14 May 1842 the first issue of *The Illustrated London News* appeared. It contained sixteen pages and thirty-two engravings. They covered the war in Afghanistan; a train crash

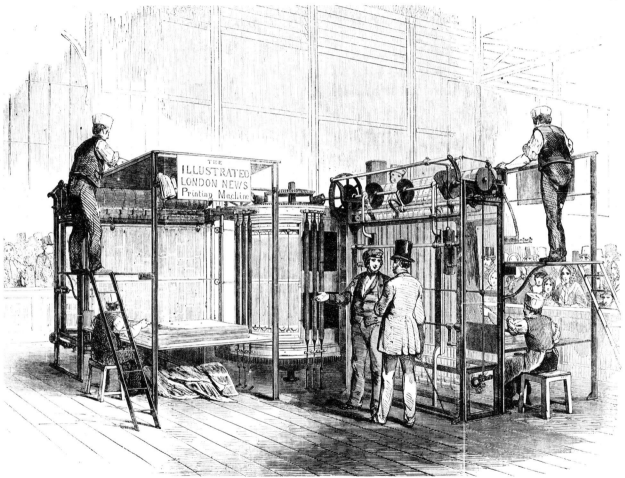

in France; a fire in Germany; a 'most fearful and fatal steam-boat explosion'
on the waters of the Chesapeake; a survey of the candidates for the American
presidency; Alderman Sir Peter Laurie's characteristically rude and facetious
dismissal of a complaint that he had slandered the owner of a matrimonial
agency; and a fancy dress ball at Buckingham Palace in which Prince Albert
appeared in the character of Edward III and the Queen as the 'noble hearted

and tender Philippa'. There were lengthy crime reports; shorter theatre and book reviews; notes on horticulture and fashion; accounts of the doings of 'the Court and Haut Ton'; a description of the exhibition of sculptures at the Royal Academy; a list of births, marriages and deaths, and of the winners at the Newmarket Second Spring Meeting. There were three pages of advertisements, recommending Barker's newly-invented razor paper, Smith's quinine tonic, Duval's apparatus for medicated baths, Godfrey's extract of elderflowers for ladies' complexions, Madame Bernard's 'treatment of the human hair' in which she removed 'the causes of baldness however inveterate or of long standing', and numerous other commodities, from a manual on the art of taxidermy, to *The Young Lady's Book*, a compendium of 'every graceful and improving Pursuit, Exercise and Accomplishment that contributes to the Accomplished English Gentlewoman'. There was a programme of the songs to be sung by Mr Wilson on Whit Monday at the Music Hall, Store Street, Bedford Square; and an announcement of a 'View of the Battle of Waterloo' to be seen at the Panorama, Leicester Square.

The price of this 'most varied publication' was sixpence; and its success was immediate and complete. The first issue sold 26,000 copies. Circulation soon rose to 40,000 and before the end of the year to 60,000. Sales reached 130,000 in 1851 after the paper had published drawings of Joseph Paxton's designs for the Crystal Palace before even Prince Albert had seen them. The next year, after a special issue was devoted to the funeral of the Duke of Wellington, sales rose to 150,000; and in 1855, partly due to the successful reproduction of Roger Fenton's photographs of the Crimean War and the abolition of the newspaper tax, they rose to 200,000 copies a week. By 1863 well over 300,000 copies were being sold.

In 1838 working-class societies all over the country demanded 'The People's Charter', whose six points were annual parliaments, universal male suffrage, equal electoral districts, the removal of the property qualification for MPs, the secret ballot and the payment of MPs. The movement gained momentum in 1842 when a petition with over three million signatures was presented to the Commons. In this riot at Salter Hebble, Halifax in August 1842, troops were called in to suppress the Chartists

There were several attempts on the Queen's life during the early years of her reign. This engraving shows an incident that took place in 1842, when the would-be assassin pointed a gun at the Queen and Albert as they drove in her carriage in the Park. When Victoria came to the throne in 1837, the esteem of the Crown was at a very low ebb, but these attacks and the Queen's courage brought her overwhelming popularity

These are astonishing figures. The circulation of *The Times*, in 1861, when the price was 3d., was no more than 70,000; the *Daily News* had only 6,000 daily readers; the *Morning Post* a mere 4,500. A Sunday newspaper like *Reynolds's Weekly News*, containing salacious stories and gossipy melodramas, sold far more copies than this, but, even so, not nearly as many as *The Illustrated London News* which was unrivalled in any class. Competitors appeared only to disappear or to be absorbed. Andrew Spottiswoode started a rival paper, the *Pictorial Times*, on which he lost £20,000 before selling it to Ingram. Henry Vizetelly left to begin his own paper, the *Illustrated Times*, which was also sold to Ingram and then suppressed. Numerous other publishers brought out periodicals whose names were already forgotten before the century was over; while the presses of *The Illustrated London News*, whose excellent paper came from Ingram's own mill, rolled on majestically.

Albert Edward, Queen Victoria's eldest son, was born on 9 November 1841. He was christened in the following January at an impressive ceremony in St George's Chapel, Windsor. This engraving was taken from a painting by Hayter

The most talented writers were employed – Shirley Brooks and George Augustus Sala, Edmund Yates and T. Hall Caine, R. L. Stevenson and George Meredith, Rider Haggard, Thomas Hardy, James Barrie, Arthur Conan Doyle and Rudyard Kipling. Gifted artists such as Constantin Guys and Melton Prior were dispatched all over the world; and, after 1860, the paper was able to combine wood engraving and photography to produce illustrations engraved from details photographed directly on to the surface of a wood block.

Ingram did not live to see the results of this new process. On 8 September 1860, the paddle-steamer in which he had taken passage at Chicago for an excursion on Lake Michigan collided with another ship and sank. He and his eldest son, together with three hundred passengers, were drowned. Some years later Ingram's youngest son was killed by an elephant while on a hunting expedition in East Africa. But by then there was a talented young grandson, Bruce, to carry on his family's paper. When Bruce Ingram became editor shortly before the Queen's death, *The Illustrated London News* had provided a unique record of the age to which she had given her name.

1 The Two Nations

Soon after the first issue of *The Illustrated London News* was published, Disraeli set to work on the novel which he was to call *Sybil*. In this novel Lord Egremont is assured that Queen Victoria reigns over two nations, 'between whom there is no intercourse and no sympathy, who are as ignorant of each other's habits, thoughts and feelings, as if they were inhabitants of different planets; who are formed by different breeding, fed by different food, ordered by different manners' and governed by different laws. They are the rich and the poor.

The contrast may have been extreme. Yet the extraordinary privileges of the aristocratic rich *did* set an unbridgeable gulf between them and ordinary men. Their riches were, indeed, prodigious. Disraeli assured Queen Victoria that the Duke of Bedford, the 'wealthiest of all her subjects', had an income 'absolutely exceeding £300,000 a year'. Later on in the century the Duke of Westminster's annual income from his London property alone was more than £250,000. There were many others whose incomes were well over £100,000 a year; and income tax in 1874–6 was 2d. in the £. Their fortunes were derived from stocks and shares, from royalties on minerals or docks, in several cases from rich wives, and in almost all cases from land: few of them had less than 10,000 acres; forty-four individual landowners had more than 100,000 acres each in the 1870s; the Duke of Devonshire had 200,000; the Duke of Buccleuch had 460,000; and the Duke of Sutherland 1,358,000. These magnates lived in a style of appropriate grandeur. Lord Egremont stabled three hundred horses at Petworth. The Duke of Westminster kept forty gardeners at Eaton Hall where guests were entertained 'on a truly royal scale'. His Grace's personal bagpipers gave strident notice to the Duke of Argyll's guests when it was time to dress for dinner at Inveraray Castle. The Duke of Rutland's guests at Belvoir Castle were awakened in the morning by a military band. Several of their aristocratic kind indulged in strange, though harmless idiosyncrasies: the Duke of Sutherland – whose lavish way of living at Trentham prompted the Shah of Persia to observe to the Prince of Wales, 'Too grand for a subject. You'll have to have his head off when you come to the throne' – had an unassuageable passion for turning out with the London fire brigade which was equalled only by his enthusiasm for driving the engines of the Highland Railway. While the Duke of Portland, who always wore three pairs of socks and carried a handkerchief a yard square, had an underground tunnel a mile and a half long built between Welbeck Abbey and the nearby town of Worksop so that his curtained

The arrival of the Queen at Waddesdon Manor, the exotic mansion built in the heart of the Buckinghamshire countryside by Baron Ferdinand de Rothschild. The house took six years to build and was modelled upon the French Renaissance style; it contained sixty-seven rooms and was one of the few houses of its time to be fitted with electric light and central heating. It was filled with the magnificent objets d'art collected by Ferdinand and his sister Alice

carriage could be driven to the railway station, lifted on to the train and transported to London without his being seen.

Yet the Victorian aristocracy skilfully adapted itself to the changing conditions of the time. The lessons of the European revolutions of 1848 were not lost upon it. Nor were those of the English Chartists. The arrogance, frivolity and selfish extravagance which had characterised so many noblemen during the regency and reign of George IV, were discarded for different, more responsible and worthy attributes. 'There is no aristocracy in the world . . . which has so honourably repented,' wrote Charles Kingsley in 1862, 'which has so cheerfully asked what its duty was, that it might do it.' Even a radical politician like Richard Cobden was obliged to conclude at the same time that in his experience the upper classes had 'never stood so high in relative social and political rank'.

Certainly they contrived with marked success to hold on to their positions of power. In the 1865 House of Commons, over three quarters of the Members were connected with the peerage by marriage, descent or interest. And those of the upper classes who were not politicians, and were not occupied exclusively with the management of their estates, were likely to be administrators or directors of businesses or, at least, active in local government

In vivid contrast to the glories of Waddesdon are these sketches of slums in Birmingham, showing the overcrowded and unsanitary conditions of the courts

and recognised by their acknowledged inferiors as being worthy both of responsibility and respect.

Below the three hundred or so aristocratic families owning extensive estates were about three thousand landed gentry, some of whom had up to 10,000 acres, but the most of whom had less than 3,000. Many of them derived at least part of their income from some kind of manufacture or business, mine or quarry. Yet there were others who lived entirely on their rents and, when all their expenses had been paid, had little left for luxury or changing fashion. A survey published in 1883 suggested that a country squire with 3,500 acres and a clear rent roll of £4,750 a year would not have much more than about £1,000 net income when all his expenses had been paid. He would have various old relations, retired servants and retainers to support; the interest on mortgages to find; he would have to pay for repairs to his buildings as well as the salary of an estate agent, the fees of a solicitor, and subscriptions to the local hunt, local charities, the church and a political party. He would also be expected to forego the rents of his poorer tenants in times of hardship.

An income of £1,000, although paltry by the standards of the very rich, was nevertheless sufficient to maintain a large country house, a man servant, a cook, a gardener, perhaps a nursemaid and governess, certainly a horse and coachman and at least two housemaids. And at a time when the best meat was 9d. a lb., Dover soles 1s. 6d. the pair, rabbits 1s. each, and oysters 7d. a dozen, there was never a problem in placing good food on the dining-room table.

Not many of the squire's friends and relations, unless they had a family business such as a bank or brewery to enter, could expect to live as well as he did. Certainly there were not many parsons who could do so. There were admittedly a hundred benefices in the Church of England worth over £2,000 a year; and there were several clergymen who were also landowners. But the wealthy sporting parson was a dying breed: the one who passed Squire Osbaldeston a note under the dining-room table to the effect that their hostess was his mistress – and gave him 'some extremely odd evidence to that effect' – was a parson of the past. Most clergymen had less than £400 a year; a few had no more than £50; and they were far more likely to resemble the Rev. Patrick Brontë than the Rev. Laurence Sterne.

Army officers were no better paid than most clergymen; and it was not until the country had been shocked by the course of the Franco-Prussian War of 1870–1 that the Secretary for War, Edward Cardwell, was able to push a Bill through Parliament abolishing the long-established practice of officers purchasing their commissions. Before that, though limits had been set on the amounts that could be lawfully paid for the various ranks, money was the recognised path to promotion in a good regiment; so that few men could afford to become officers unless they had private means to supplement their meagre pay and none could hope to get on in such a regiment as the 17th Lancers for the command of which the Earl of Lucan paid £25,000.

Talented and industrious young men without private means or family connections found it less difficult to prosper in careers in medicine or law. A promising barrister could earn £5,000 a year; and such celebrated lawyers as Charles Russell were in the 1880s receiving over £15,000 a year. Incomes of these dimensions were beyond the reach of most doctors; but 'a physician who is becoming popular', so it was estimated in 1850, could count on £1,000

a year; while physicians of the standing of Sir William Jenner, who left a fortune of £375,000, could earn ten times more than that.

Jenner and his kind enjoyed social as well as professional prestige. But surgeons were of a somewhat lower caste, and a family physician with an ordinary practice would not usually expect to be treated as an equal by the squire and would not presume to consider his daughter a suitable match for the squire's son. Nor would he be asked to stay to dinner as would the fashionable London doctor whose advice was sought in most cases of grave illness. The medical profession, in fact, was a hierarchy within the larger hierarchy of the Victorian social structure.

So was the legal profession. The President of the Law Society with his grand and spacious offices in Chancery Lane and Lincoln's Inn Fields, and his membership of the Junior Carlton, or one of the other new clubs which had been built in Pall Mall for the growing numbers of the prosperous middle class, was a very different person from those solicitors whom Dickens had known when he himself was a clerk with Messrs Ellis and Blackmore and whose dingy offices, smelling of unwholesome sheep, he afterwards described in novel after novel. The clerks who worked in these offices belonged to yet another class in Victorian society which was itself again divided into different grades, the lowest of which – shabby, middle-aged copying clerks – might earn no more than the 30s. a week which a skilled workman could expect, though in the higher grades £4 or even £5 a week was not uncommon.

In all large late Victorian towns there were rows upon rows of houses occupied by men earning up to about £250 a year, an income which was sufficient to employ a maidservant at £20 a year and to lead a life of quiet respectability far removed, in spirit if not in space, from the life of the teeming poor and that 'hungry ocean of violence' which Richard Church, the son of a postman, remembers as ever appearing to threaten his peaceful suburb of clerks, minor civil servants and sober artisans in Battersea.

Below Scenes from the Electrical Exhibition held at the Crystal Palace in 1882. A drawing-room lit by electricity, and a sewing-machine driven by an electric motor

To no other people in Victorian society were the inventions of the age more useful and beneficial than they were to the lower middle classes. Sewing machines, closed cooking ranges, ready-prepared, mass-produced foods, machine-made clothes and boots, cheap soap and paraffin oil, the improvement of the postal system and the spread of gaslight all made incalculable differences to their lives. Most important of all was the advent of cheap travel.

Left The Thames Embankment first illuminated by electricity in 1879

Opposite An oil cooking stove of 1897; an advertisement from *The Graphic*

The Easiest
The Cheapest } Mode of Cooking.
The Cleanest

"Upwards of **ONE MILLION** of our Stoves in ACTUAL and SUCCESSFUL use at the present time in all parts of the World!"

The "ALBIONETTE" IS THE COOKER OF THE <u>FUTURE</u>

THE "ALBIONETTE"

THE only perfect Oil Cooking Stove, performs every Cooking operation *at one and the same time* at one-third the cost of COAL or GAS. Heat regulated to a nicety.

Lit and Extinguished in a moment. " Our Latest and Best."

The result of **25** *years' experience.*

All other Oil Stoves are now old-fashioned.

Sold by all Stores and Ironmongers. Prices from 27s. to 90s. Illustrated Catalogue free, from

Rippingille's Albion Lamp Co., BIRMINGHAM.

ORIGINAL Inventors of Oil Cookers. Contractors to H.M. Government.

London Depôt and Show-rooms: 65, HOLBORN VIADUCT, E.C.

RECEIVING LETTERS AT THE E.C. WINDOW

Activities at the General Post Office at St Martins-le-Grand in 1875. In the first scene is shown the East Central District Office, into which the City letters are posted direct. The next scene shows the Inland Lobby, the point of arrival for provincial mailbags brought in from railway stations. In the third scene, the letters are sorted and made up into bags for dispatch, and in the fourth scene the letters are being 'faced' so that they can be read easily during sorting

MAKING-UP AT 7-57½

24

RECEIVING PROVINCIAL BAGS IN THE INLAND LOBBY

FACING LETTERS

25

Left The arrival of frozen meat from Australia at the South-west India dock in Millwall, London. The invention of 'dry air refrigerators' in the late 1870s brought an abundant supply of fresh meat into Britain, but this development hit hard the home cattle farmers, and helped to bring about the agricultural depression of the last years of the nineteenth century

SUGG'S "ALADDIN" READING LAMP

PATENT (SELF GOVERNING)

3 FT OF GAS PER HOUR.

EQUAL TO 16 CANDLES.

SUPERIOR TO THE ELECTRIC LIGHT.

FOR THE OFFICE, STUDIO, LIBRARY, WORKROOM.

PRICE - 25/-
COMPLETE AS SHEWN

1/4 FULL SIZE.

BRILLIANT SILENT WHITE LIGHT

GRAND HOTEL B⁰⁰ˢ CHARING ✠ W.C.

Left A gas reading lamp, much vaunted as superior to electric light; an advertisement from an 1887 edition of *The Illustrated London News*

Opposite A telephone exchange in London in 1883. The upper picture shows the switchroom of a central office worked by a slipper board system, while the lower scene shows a switchroom worked by the peg board system

26

27

'Omnibus life in London', from
a painting by W. M. Egley, 1859

28

De Tivoli's patent omnibus,
which first made its appearance
in the London streets in 1860.
This particular omnibus ran
from the Great Western Railway
terminus at Paddington to
London Bridge

Few Victorians could afford their own carriages, so that the increase in numbers of horse-drawn omnibuses, which had first been seen in 1829, and the subsequent lowering of fares, were warmly welcomed. By 1855 20,000 people were being transported to work by omnibus every day in London alone; and five years later many of these commuters were travelling in De Tivoli's patent omnibuses which *The Illustrated London News* described as having 'separate well-ventilated compartments for one person each, a position at the back being left undivided to contain four second-class passengers', the other passengers sitting on the roof.

The bicycle did not appear until the 1870s; and even then it was often a heavy, clumsy structure little better than the model which a Staffordshire farm labourer bought for 2s. 6d. 'with a wooden frame and handlebars, but no chains or pedals, you simply pushed it along the ground with your feet'. The first commercially successful 'safety' bicycle, the Rover, built at Coventry by J. K. Starley, did not come on to the market until 1886; and J. B. Dunlop's pneumatic tyre was not patented until 1888.

By then the old horse-drawn trams had been replaced, first by steam-driven and then electric trams; the underground railways, whose first line had been opened between Paddington and the City in 1863, were being developed and extended; and Gottfried Daimler had perfected his high-

Above left The joys and problems of riding the penny farthing bicycle, from an 1882 edition of *The Illustrated Sporting and Dramatic News*

speed internal combustion engine. In England an old law, not repealed until 1896, prohibited mechanical vehicles being driven on public roads at more than four miles an hour behind a man carrying a red flag, and this did much to inhibit the development of a national motor-car industry. But before the death of the Queen – who possessed an electric motor-car capable of covering forty miles on one charge at twelve miles an hour – small cars, which could reach speeds of twenty miles an hour and could be run for about 4d. a mile,

Above The first electric tram-line in Europe was opened at Northfleet in Kent in 1889. This was run on the 'series system' whereby the current was generated at a central station and sent through the line, thus being taken up by the cars as they ran along and passed through them before returning to the station

were available for less than £200. For most people, though, no form of transport was yet as important as the railway train.

'What a gulf between now and then!' exclaims one of Thackeray's characters. '*Then* was the old world . . . But your railroad starts a new era . . . We who lived before railways and survive out of the ancient world, are like Father Noah and his family out of the Ark.'

Traffic jams are not only a phenomenon of the twentieth century. This scene took place in Park Lane in December 1864, and among the tangle is an omnibus from the Paddington to Victoria route, a carriage and pair, a hansom cab, a costermonger's donkey cart and a farmer's herd of sheep and cattle

33

Left The trial-trip in 1862 of the Metropolitan railway, the first underground line, which ran between Paddington and Victoria Street in the City

Opposite Queen Victoria enjoyed travelling by train and made her first train journey in June 1842 from Paddington to Windsor. Her luxurious private carriage was built by the London and North-west Railway in 1869, and she used this for her trips up to Balmoral. In this illustration of 1879 the Queen is shown looking out of her carriage as the train crosses the Tay Bridge at Dundee

Below The Arnold carriage, a motor-car of 1896

The building of
Blackfriars railway
bridge in 1864. In
the foreground is
shown the temporary
timber bridge built
across the Thames,
and to the right, the
actual railway bridge
in construction. This
bridge was to carry
the railway from the
Elephant and Castle
across the Thames to
the Blackfriars
terminus. In the
background can be
seen St Paul's
Cathedral, St
Martin's Ludgate,
and *The Times*' offices
in Printing House
Square

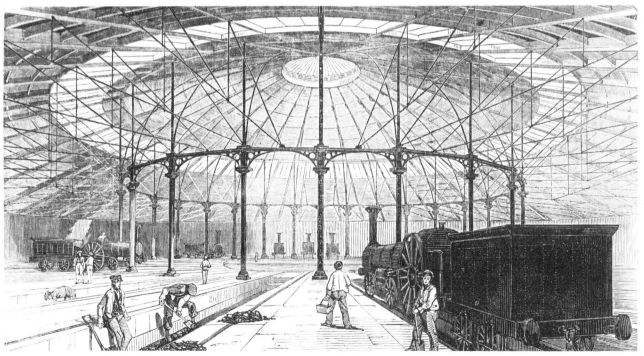

Above The advent of the railway transformed both the cities and the countryside of Victorian Britain. This view of Leeds from Holbeck junction, drawn in 1868, shows how the railway dominated the landscape

Left The Round House at Chalk Farm, which was used by the North-western Railway as an engine house and giant turn-table. This building is now used as a theatre-cum-concert hall

By the time of Thackeray's death in 1863, railways had certainly transformed the whole tenor of English life as well as the English landscape. Yet it was no more than a generation earlier that the 'railway mania' had begun to sweep across the country. Armies of men who had originally worked on canals and were hence known as navigators – or, more commonly, navvies – had marched across the country, with picks and shovels, wheelbarrows and lanterns on their backs, to prepare the ground for the long, wide tracks, to dig cuttings, to excavate tunnels, to build up embankments. They were a rough, tough lot, often drunk, frequently fighting, working hard, followed by old women who did their cooking and by younger women who were their concubines. They were well paid in comparison with other labourers, receiving 24s. a week for unskilled work; but it was a dangerous life: 32 men were killed while digging the Woodhead tunnel on the line between Sheffield and Manchester, and 540 men were injured, many of them seriously.

While navvies sweated by day and drank by night, fortunes were made and lost. George Stephenson, builder of the famous *Rocket* and of the Liverpool and Manchester Railway, was born the son of a poor colliery fireman and died, rich and respected, at a large country house in Derbyshire. Stephenson's protégé, Thomas Brassey, contractor for the Great Northern Railway among others, died in 1870 worth many million pounds. George Hudson, the ebullient Yorkshire 'Railway King' and chairman of the Midland Railway, who became a millionaire, a national figure, and a

Member of Parliament, was forced to flee to the Continent, heavily in debt, leaving investors in companies he had promoted with losses totalling £50 million.

Despite Hudson's ruin and disgrace, railways proliferated as fast as ever. By 1852 there were only three important English towns – Hereford, Yeovil and Weymouth – without a railway station; and by 1875 nearly five million passengers were being transported by rail each year.

At first the prospect of being driven along an iron track at great speed was too much for many would-be travellers to contemplate. When it was learned that the carriages on the Woolwich–London line would travel at eighteen

The Crumlin viaduct, built to extend the railway from Newport to Taff Vale, thus opening up the mineral districts of Monmouthshire and Glamorganshire. At the time of its construction, in the 1850s, the Crumlin viaduct was the largest structure of its kind in the world

miles an hour, a writer in the *Quarterly Review* protested, 'We should as soon expect the people of Woolwich to be fired off upon one of Congreve's ricochet rockets as trust themselves to the mercy of such a machine going at such a rate.' In those days thirty miles an hour was still considered a fast speed. And many of the smaller lines did not presume to such velocity. The Eastern Counties line was one of them; so notoriously slow was it, indeed, that a robust youth of sixteen, discovered to be travelling at half-price, pleaded that he had been under twelve when the train started! By 1848, however, the *Great Britain* was roaring into London at more than a mile a minute.

Opposite First-, second- and
third-class passengers on their
way to the Epsom Races in 1847

Below The Great Western Royal
Hotel, built next door to
Paddington Station in 1852. This
structure, based on the Louis XIV
style, was at the time of its
opening the most luxurious
hotel in Britain

While speeds improved, the safety of the passengers did not. There were
fifteen times as many fatal accidents in England as there were in Germany,
many of them the fault of the passengers themselves who were constantly
attempting to board moving trains, jumping off to pick up their hats, sitting
on the tops of the carriages and falling over the sides of the open, seatless
trucks which were the only form of accommodation at first provided for third-
class passengers, who were nevertheless charged at the rate of 1½d. a mile.

The railways found many victims other than these. In all the big towns,
particularly in London, tens of thousands of people were displaced and their
homes demolished by companies who did not always have the means to
rehouse them adequately. And still more demolition was carried out when it
was decided that the earlier stations, like Isambard Kingdom Brunel's
Paddington and the London and Birmingham Railway's terminus in Euston

Square, were not sufficiently central. The more modern London termini were subsequently built closer to the heart of the city at even greater cost to its inhabitants. The Italianate structures of Blackfriars and Broad Street stations; John Hawkshaw's Charing Cross station; Sir George Gilbert Scott's vast Gothic edifice at St Pancras and the extensive buildings erected for the London, Chatham and Dover Railway on the Grosvenor Estate and renamed after the Queen, all appeared between 1863 and 1886. At the same time, impressive railway stations were being built in the large towns of the provinces, many of them by that gifted railway architect, Sir William Tite, and most of them provided with that indispensable adjunct of the railway station, the railway hotel.

Unknown in England before the advent of the railway, the hotel was a Victorian innovation. And, although there were plenty of Englishmen who gloomily complained of the departure of the old coaching inn, foreigners were soon speaking well of the comfort and cuisine of many English hotels, particularly those at Charing Cross, St Pancras, and, most warmly of all, of the hotel next door to Paddington Station, the Great Western Royal Hotel, which was, at the time of its opening, the biggest and most luxurious hotel in the country. Even that most fastidious of *bon viveurs*, the Prince of Wales, said that the Langham, whose opening he attended in 1865, was worthy of comparison with the Astoria, New York; and that the cuisine at the Carlton, where Georges-Auguste Escoffier, formerly of the Savoy, presided over a synod of sixty cooks and first introduced menus *à la carte*, was nonpareil.

2 Town Life

In 1842, although England was still a predominantly rural country, people were leaving the land in a steady stream; and, helped by the railways, the towns were growing fast. By 1851, for the first time, they contained more people than the country. In that year the total population of Britain was just under 21,000,000 of whom over 2,500,000 lived in Greater London, the biggest city in the Western world. Manchester's population was 303,000, Birmingham's 233,000 and Glasgow's 345,000. By 1881, when over twice as many people lived in the towns as in the country, there were twenty-six cities with more than 100,000 inhabitants, Glasgow, Birmingham, Liverpool and Manchester all having more than 400,000.

But although the towns were growing fast, the wages of urban workers were not. Farm labourers earning less than 10s. a week in the 1840s often found it difficult to earn much more in a town. Factory hands in the textile industry, for example, commonly took home less than 15s. a week; and there were many other industries whose rates of pay were not much better than this. Indeed, in those days most labouring people at some time or other in their lives knew what real hunger was. By the middle of the 1860s, however, wages began to improve; and in 1867 it was calculated that, apart from unskilled labourers and workers in some peculiarly depressed trades, the majority of men in regular employment were earning more than £1 a week. The gradual upward trend in wage levels continued throughout the late 1860s and early 1870s. Thereafter, however, there was a slow falling back in standards of living; and in the 1890s Charles Booth, a Liverpool merchant who made a detailed study of the labouring class in London, reckoned that a third of the population was in poverty with wages of 25s. or 26s. at the most for a large family.

What these sums could buy was very little. 'A decent man earning 25s. a week will give 20s. to his wife,' the vicar of a poor parish reported to one of Booth's investigators. 'She ought to be able to – because in many cases she does – feed four children, dress herself, and pay rent out of this. The 5s. is kept by the man for his beer and tobacco.' The rent for two rooms and a boxroom might be 6s. a week; 4s. or so might go on clothes, heating and medicine; most of the rest would be spent on food. And while a respectable family such as this rarely went hungry – for 3s. would buy 1 quart of milk, 2 lbs. of bacon, 1 dozen eggs and 1 lb. of cheese – there was little left over for the kind of extras that a highly skilled worker – a compositor, mason or watchmaker – would be able to afford with his £3 or £3 10s. Moreover,

Above Manchester in 1876: a
bird's eye view from the tower
of the new Town Hall

Above right Dwellings of
Manchester operatives in 1862.
The dire poverty of these
industrial workers can be seen all
too clearly

clothes and boots had to be chosen with an eye to their durability rather than
their elegance; and if more was spent on drink than a family could afford – as
it so often was – regular visits had to be paid to the neighbourhood pawnbroker.

Temperance workers estimated that in the middle of the century more was
spent every year on drink than on rent – an average of £3 for each person.
Official figures tended to confirm this and indicated that, in the 1870s, the
people were drinking more than ever – about ten pints of spirits, four pints of
wine and 275 pints of beer each year for every man, woman and child. The
problem was aggravated by the common practice – eventually prohibited by
law – of paying workers' wages in a public house in whose profits the
employers had an interest. In the early 1840s coal-backers on the London
docks, for example, had to spend as much as half their wages in dockside
taverns, otherwise they were given no work. In most other unskilled trades a
man who did not drink was considered an outcast; and even in skilled trades
there were numerous occasions, such as the promotion of an apprentice,
when it was traditional for a worker to stand treat to all his colleagues
whether or not he could afford it. It was not surprising, therefore, that no
public house was far away from a pawnbroker.

Some employers refused to allow their men to drink and instantly dis-
missed any found doing so. One of these was William Fairbarn, owner of a
Lancashire engineering works, whose determination to regulate his employees' conduct went so far as to admonish them if they were seen appearing
ill-dressed in the streets on a Sunday. Another was Sir Titus Salt, a Bradford
manufacturer of autocratic temper, outside whose huge mill on the banks of
the river Aire a notice was displayed forbidding his workers to touch any
alcohol, even beer. There were compensations for the workers of Saltaire,
however. Sir Titus provided over eight hundred good houses for his men and
their families; he also provided them with a school, a chapel, a park, an
infirmary, public baths and a public dining-hall.

Left One of the most
characteristic scenes of the life of
the poor, the pawnbroker's shop

Below A temperance meeting
held at Sadler's Wells Theatre in
1854, as drawn by George
Cruikshank

Above Model farm buildings and workshops built by the Marquis of Bath for his estate workers at Longleat in Wiltshire in 1859

Although the scope of Salt's paternalism was exceptional, there were numerous other employers who, in return for an obedient, orderly work force, were prepared to interest themselves in the welfare of their men, to pay them relatively good wages, to provide pensions for them when they were too old to work and for their widows when they died. Yet, according to Engels, who was appalled by their conditions in Manchester, the great majority of workers in the 1840s had to live with the fear that, though they might have the means of existence today, it was very uncertain whether they would tomorrow. If they were not liable to be put out of work by the weather or by a trade recession, they were always likely to fall ill or to suffer from some industrial injury for which no employer was obliged to accept responsibility. And for many of them such misfortunes were an ever-present danger. There were, for example, in 1867, 230,000 miners in England and Wales, most of whom were working in pits where conditions were not only almost as unpleasant and unhealthy as they had ever been, but where innovations had been very slow to gain acceptance. Steam engines were only very gradually substituted for horse-winches; while the huge, unwieldy wicker 'corves', raised by hempen ropes, were even more slowly replaced by iron 'cages' and wire cables; and it was not until 1860 that the first fan was seen in Durham instead of the primitive methods of ventilating pits by means of a vast furnace near the base of the upcast shaft. Not for several years after that did the fan

become universal; nor did Davy's safety lamp immediately put an end to the use of candles and the consequent risk of an explosion of firedamp. A thousand miners were still killed each year in the 1870s; and many more lost limbs or suffered from that inflammation of the lungs known as 'black spittle'.

Other industries were equally disinclined to adapt themselves to innovations. Nasmyth's steam-hammer, invented in 1839, was very slow to gain acceptance in the ironworking industry; and Henry Bessemer's announcement in 1856 of his new steel-making process was greeted warily and regarded sceptically for many years, while demand for wrought-iron continued to increase. The clothing industry was quite as reluctant to make use of the sewing-machine; and, long after the machine's first appearance, the manufacture of coats, like the making of boots, remained a pure handicraft. The position was much the same in the Midlands' hosiery trade in which nearly all the 120,000 people employed in 1862 were still working in their own cottages or in small frame-shops. Most lace-workers in and around Nottingham also worked at home for very low rates of pay. So did most silk-workers who were among the lowest paid men in the whole country, earning in an average week in the middle of the 1860s no more than 12s.

Above London grew rapidly throughout the nineteenth century. As the central areas became overcrowded, so the suburb areas were developed in every direction. These sketches show the development of the western suburbs, swallowing up the villages of Kensington, Fulham and Barons Court in the 1880s

Right Pitmen at work in the south Durham coalfields in 1871. On the right the small boy, known as a 'putter', will drive the pit pony with the loaded tub back to the bottom of the pit shaft. On the left, the hewers are digging out the coal

Below Cotton workers at Dean Mills near Manchester in 1851. This scene shows the doubling room where the thread is doubled to produce fine thread for the manufacture of lace

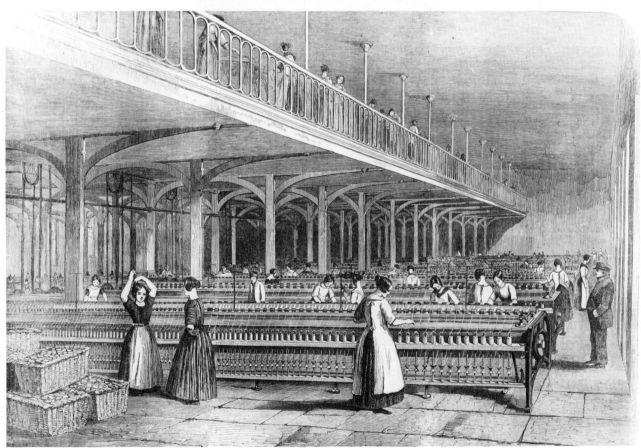

Ironworkers casting a large
cylinder at the Canal Works in
Poplar in 1863. The cylinder was
to form part of the steam engines
for a steamer ship of the P&O
Company

Factory workers were better paid; but although conditions were slowly improving, factories were usually far from pleasant places in which to work. Few of them were as large as those forbidding Lancashire cotton mills, built on several storeys with row upon row of small-paned windows behind whose grimy glass, steam-driven looms made a deafening roar in the foul and gaslit air. Admittedly, the big iron works of South Wales employed an average of 650 men each in 1870–1; and a ship-building yard might employ a thousand, there being a boom in big iron ships: the ill-fated *Great Eastern*, launched in 1858, was followed in 1860 by the more successful *Warrior*, the first British ironclad warship which was half as big again as the biggest three-decker in the world. After the *Warrior* there came a succession of iron ships all carefully depicted in *The Illustrated London News* – from the *Devastation* and the *Thunderer* (the first large iron warships to abandon sails), the *Collingwood* (the first to be built entirely of steel), and the *Rodney* (completed in 1888 when the *Devastation* was obsolete), to the *Royal Sovereign*, launched in 1891, the earliest battleship to cost more than £1 million.

Few factories, however, employed anything like the number of men to be found in a ship-building yard, only the very largest having more than two hundred workers and most having ten men or less. Yet the smaller factories were usually quite as uncongenial as the larger ones – indeed, were often more so, the Factory Acts being more easily evaded in smaller workshops –

Warrior, the first British
ironclad warship, which was half
as big again as the largest
three-decker in the world

while the monotony and drudgery of the work was common to them all.
Even so, the factory worker was frequently far better placed than those
millions of workers who were beyond the protection of the Factory Acts
altogether.

Domestic servants, the largest single category of labour in Victorian
England, were entirely at the mercy of their employers. So were shop
assistants whose working day was almost as long. So were most clerks and
office workers whose numbers were increasing year by year and whose
conditions of work in the middle of the century were a good deal less comfortable than many manual workers supposed. The clerical staff of one Lancashire mill, for instance, were required to clean their own offices before prayers
every morning; and although they were provided with a stove, they were
advised to 'bring four pounds of coal each during cold weather'.

The houses in which these workers lived were not likely to be much more
comfortable than the places in which they worked. In Manchester, so Engels
maintained, almost all the 350,000 working people lived 'in wretched, damp,
filthy cottages'. And housing elsewhere was little better. A Quaker alderman
condemned whole quarters of Birmingham as a rotting, dilapidated warren
of 'bowing roofs, tottering chimneys, tumbledown and often disused shops,
heaps of bricks, broken windows and coarse, rough pavements, damp and
sloppy'. For the sake of cheapness thousands of cottages, particularly in the

Opposite The communal water tank in St Giles-in-the-Fields, one of the most squalid slum areas of London. Barrow boys, en route from Covent Garden market, would refresh their wares in this backstreet court

north, were built back-to-back with privies in front and ashpits in the street: there were eight thousand dwellings like this in Nottingham alone. Thousands more were built round ill-cleaned and ill-ventilated courts whose occupants were obliged to share a common privy and a common tap: in mid-century Liverpool 55,000 people were housed in this way. As late as 1881 almost a quarter of Glasgow's population had no more than one room in which to live, and almost half had no more than two. In Leeds uncounted numbers of people, mostly Irish immigrants, slept with pigs in damp, undrained cellars. London was as bad as anywhere. Hippolyte Taine, who had seen the bad quarters of Marseilles and Paris, thought them not nearly as bad as some poor districts of London, notably Shadwell, which he saw in 1871.

Several industrialists put up decent cottages which sprawled in long, red-brick lines from the factory gates towards the open countryside; and towards the end of the century, these – like the houses built by W. H. Lever at Port Sunlight and George Cadbury at Bournville Village – had adequate drains, a water supply, and even gas. Various philanthropists and housing associations also provided healthy and reasonably comfortable, if rather intimidating, blocks of dwellings for working-class occupants: the Model Dwellings built by George Peabody, an American merchant living in London, were representative examples. Nevertheless, overcrowding in squalid conditions, particularly in the north, remained the lot of thousands of poor families throughout the Queen's reign.

In every big town, however, often towering above the houses of the people, were public edifices of increasing size, impressiveness and dignity. More building was carried out in England in the nineteenth century, in fact, than in all the centuries that had preceded it. Town halls and law courts, hospitals and schools, museums and galleries, government offices and banks, university colleges and libraries, clubs, hotels and theatres all appeared in such numbers, and in such a variety of styles, that the artists of *The Illustrated London News* were kept busy drawing them, week in, week out, first in one county, then in the next. There were splendid Greek buildings like H. L. Elmes' St George's Hall, Liverpool; there were English Renaissance buildings like T. G. Jackson's Examination Schools, Oxford; there were Byzantine buildings like the Roman Catholic cathedral in Westminster for which J. F. Bentley provided plans in the 1890s. Above all, there were Gothic buildings – Tudor Gothic palaces such as Sir Charles Barry's Houses of Parliament which, with embellishments by Augustus Pugin, was completed in 1865; immense stone Gothic structures in the thirteenth-century castellated style, like G. E. Street's Law Courts in the Strand; and huge red-brick Gothic offices on the lines of the Prudential Assurance Building in Holborn by Alfred Waterhouse who also produced the Metropole Hotel at Brighton and St Paul's School, Hammersmith. There were banks which C. R. Cockerell designed to resemble classical temples; railway stations and prisons that looked like medieval castles; and a new Scotland Yard to which Norman Shaw gave the appearance of an early Renaissance French *château*. George Basevi's classical Fitzwilliam Museum in the Corinthian order at Cambridge was followed by Cockerell's Ashmolean Museum in the Ionic order at Oxford. Sir George Gilbert Scott provided a medieval memorial to the Protestant martyrs, Latimer, Ridley and Cranmer, at Oxford; and in London a memorial of intricate craftsmanship in white Italian marble, bronze, wrought iron, granite, agate, onyx, jasper, cornelian and crystal to Prince Albert.

Overleaf Scenes of distress in the East End of London in 1886. In the top left-hand corner, a woman is shown making sacks at less than 2d per hour, and in the centre is a scene from a common lodging house. The lower pictures show dockers desperate for work, and 'a good type' of East End court in Shadwell

The size and style of buildings were often influenced by considerations neither practical nor aesthetic. When George Gilbert Scott entered the competition organised in 1856 for new government offices in Whitehall his Gothic designs were at first accepted. But Whig advocates of the classical style – warmly supported by Lord Palmerston and angrily attacked by their political opponents in both Houses of Parliament – condemned the Gothic taste as too much associated with conservatism and with the High Church movement; and so orders were given for an Italian design to be submitted instead. Scott endeavoured to arrange a compromise by proposing a Byzantine building in the style of the early Venetian palaces. But Palmerston would have nothing to do with such 'a regular mongrel affair'. Against his better judgment, Scott was compelled to produce the Italianate Foreign and War Offices which were finally begun five years after the competition had been held.

Rivalries of a different kind led to the building of a town hall at Leeds at far greater expense than had originally been proposed. For, when the Mayor of Bradford announced that his city's recently constructed St George's Hall was the 'best known specimen' of such a building in all England, eleven feet wider than Birmingham Town Hall, even loftier than Exeter Hall in London and capable of containing concert audiences of over three thousand people, the merchants of Leeds were much irritated by the claims. They commissioned a young Yorkshire architect, Cuthbert Brodrick, to build for them a fine town hall of which they could be just as proud. When the Queen came to Leeds

Model dwellings constructed in Shadwell by George Peabody, a philanthropic American merchant who lived in London. Despite their grimness, these buildings were a considerable improvement on the squalid backstreet courts in the poor districts of London's East End

Leeds Town Hall built by
Cuthbert Brodrick and
completed in 1858. The
merchants of Leeds were
determined to outshine all
possible rivals and their huge
municipal edifice exceeded the
dimensions of similar structures
in London, Birmingham and
Bradford

for the official opening in 1858 Brodrick's massive classical structure was
certainly an imposing sight. It covered an area of 5,600 square yards, was
longer than London's Guildhall, higher than the town hall in Birmingham
and wider than Westminster Hall. That it was larger than St George's Hall,
Bradford, the citizens of Leeds had no need to be assured.

3 Country Life

'English farming, taken as a whole,' wrote a French agriculturist in 1854, 'is at this day the first in the world; and is about to become even better.' Farming methods, other observers confirmed, were more advanced than those employed almost anywhere else in Europe: crops were plentiful; breeds were sound and strong; horses, rather than oxen, pulled almost every plough. Farms were far bigger than they were on the Continent, the average being over 100 acres in extent, half the country's whole farmland being in holdings of about 200 acres.

Most of these holdings were rented from local landowners with whom the farmers might mix in the hunting field or at the cattle show but from whom they were separated by as wide a social gulf as separated the prosperous solicitor from his ill-paid clerk. The larger farmer, living in a comfortable house with servants inside and labourers in the fields outside, was a man of some consequence; but he had no pretensions to being a gentleman. He did not take much interest in local affairs; he usually steered clear of the parson; and had little use for education. The smaller farmer was obliged to work a great deal harder, finding it as much as he could do to look after his land and animals with the help of his family and perhaps one or two hired labourers.

Left Carrots being gathered and bunched ready for transport to Covent Garden market. This scene was sketched in a Kensington market garden in 1861

Opposite The Cornmarket in Mark Lane in the City of London in 1842

Overleaf A demonstration of steam ploughing which took place near Louth in Lincolnshire in 1857. The traction engine, with three double ploughs, was capable of ploughing eight acres in a ten-hour day, while six single ploughs and eighteen horses would plough only four and a half acres in the same time

At the beginning of the period the wages of these labourers were low; their hours were long; and their work was extremely laborious. Machinery was gradually coming into use; steam ploughs began to be seen in certain areas. But farmers were a conservative breed; they mostly preferred the scythe, the sickle and the flail which their fathers and grandfathers had used before them; while the labourers themselves feared the introduction of new inventions as a threat to their livelihood and had been known to smash threshing machines in the manner of the Luddites.

Fowler's patent four-furrow steam plough, as shown at the International Exhibition of 1876

Hornsby's portable steam engine being used to drive a threshing machine in 1851

In the early 1850s wages in some areas were as low as 6s. a week. Labourers were usually hired by the year and lived together in a primitive cottage provided by their employer with an elderly woman to look after them and cook their food. Some labourers, particularly those who had worked in the north, remembered being contented and well-fed with 'any amount of bread and bacon, and plenty of home-brewed beer, and, in the winter, a sure, drowsy place by the kitchen fire'. But most recalled less happy times; rising at dawn in cold and leaking cottages to put on clothes still wet from the previous day's rain; working until sunset for a paltry wage; eating bread and potatoes, with an occasional piece of bacon and an apple dumpling; often going to bed hungry. It was estimated that two million people in Britain lived almost entirely on potatoes. In Ireland four million did so; and when the Irish crop failed hardship and famine were inevitable. In 1846 the whole Irish crop was blighted and hundreds of thousands of people died either of starvation or of the fevers that attended malnutrition.

During the 1870s conditions began gradually to improve in most areas in Britain as Joseph Arch's agricultural trade union became effective. But then, towards the end of that decade, there came the depression. In 1875 there was an exceptionally wet summer, as there was the next year and the next. In 1877 there was also an outbreak of rinderpest. Yet another wet summer in 1878 was followed in 1879 by the worst and wettest summer that most farmers could remember, this time accompanied by an outbreak of liver-rot in sheep. Four years later there was a widespread and violent epidemic of

Poverty and terrible living conditions were not limited to the great industrial cities. This scene of the interior of a cottage in Dorset in 1846 shows the misery of agricultural workers. The wages of these workers rarely exceeded seven shillings a week

The agricultural depression of
the 1840s caused grave distress
in Ireland, where hundreds of
thousands of people died of
starvation. This scene from
Galway in 1842 shows the
starving attacking a potato store

The interior of a mud cabin in
Kildare in 1870. In this
particular room lived four
people. They had no bedstead or
bedding, but slept in their
clothes on the bare ground. The
only furniture was a rickety
table and a broken bench with
an iron pot and kettle, and two
or three cups

In the 1870s Joseph Arch began to build up a trade union of agricultural labourers. In 1876, a conference of delegates was held in London to back up demands for equal electoral reform in the country as in the towns. In this scene, delegates are shown signing the petition: in fact this electoral reform was not passed until 1884

foot-and-mouth disease. During these years the growth of railways in the United States, the spread of farm machinery there and the increasing cheapness of ocean-going steamer transport combined to make it possible for American farmers to export vast quantities of prairie-wheat. The price of English wheat plummeted and soon almost half the country's grain, nearly all of which had previously been supplied at home, was coming from abroad. In the wake of the wheat came imports of frozen meat, of live cattle and of a cheap substitute for butter from Holland. Farm wages fell sharply; farmers went bankrupt; whole tracts of land were abandoned to birds of prey; almost 100,000 labourers left the land to find work in the towns; and over a million people emigrated. The great landowners spoke gloomily of ruin – and found comfort in sport.

C.J. STANILAND.

The agricultural
depression of the
1870s and 1880s
caused many
thousands of people
to emigrate. This
illustration shows life
below decks on an
emigrant ship in 1887

To many a Victorian country gentleman hunting was a way of life, as it was to the celebrated Thomas Assheton Smith, that fearless and popular Master of the Quorn, who was still hunting four times a week in his eightieth year. It was fortunate for Assheton Smith that he owned a Welsh slate quarry as well as a Hampshire estate, for hunting was an expensive business even then, with hounds to be fed and kennelled, with hunt servants to be paid and provided with livery, with coverts, gates and bridges to be maintained and with horses to be stabled. But there was never a lack of men who would have given their eye teeth to be appointed Master of Fox Hounds, and to head the list of subscribers to the local hunt. ''Unting is all that's worth living for,' said John Jorrocks, the cheerful, vulgar, rich London grocer who, to his delighted astonishment, was invited to become Master of the impoverished hunt of *Handley Cross*. 'All time is lost wot is not spent in 'unting.' It was a sentiment that thousands of squires wholeheartedly endorsed.

Hunting changed little during the Victorian period; but shooting was transformed. The flint-lock became a weapon of the past; the muzzle-loader gave way to the breech-loader; and beaters took the place of spaniels. Gone were the days when Squire George Osbaldeston, another Master of the Quorn, could kill a hundred pheasants with a hundred shots from his

Above Lawn meet of the West Norfolk hounds at Sandringham in 1886. The Prince of Wales is depicted on the left

Opposite Breech-loading shotguns being used on a partridge shoot in 1895

WATCHING.

DEATH OF THE LURCHER.

THE FIGHT.

'flint and steel of eighteen bore' as the birds clattered out of the thick stubble in front of his feet. Now the fashion was for grand *battues* conducted on the lines of military operations in which the slaughter was immense.

To maintain a good supply of game required both money and skill; and landowners, who employed about three thousand gamekeepers between them, talked endlessly of the problems as well as the pleasures of a shoot, castigating the depredations of poachers and bewailing the relaxation of the game laws. Not so much eager talk seems to have been devoted to fishing; but in many quarters racing was a never-ending topic of interest. The Ascot meeting had been established since the beginning of the eighteenth century. The Derby and the Oaks at Epsom and the St Leger at Doncaster were also of eighteenth-century origin; and the annual meeting at Goodwood began in 1802. Thereafter the sport had become more and more popular, many further classics, including the Grand National, the Cesarewitch and the Cambridgeshire, being run for the first time in Victoria's reign. Thanks largely to the determined efforts of Lord George Bentinck, racing had also become rather less corrupt; fraudulence, the doping and substitution of horses being markedly more uncommon than in the time of George IV.

Derby Day at Epsom was still, however, as raffish as it had always been, and far more unruly than Frith's painting suggests. Amongst the tipsters and the acrobats, the superannuated jockeys and whores, were scores of shifty eyes on the look-out for trouble or an unguarded pocket or purse – the kind

Opposite Poachers apprehended by gamekeepers

Below In 1896, the Prince of Wales won his first Derby with his horse Persimmon. His victory was tremendously popular, and the crowds gave him a tumultuous welcome when he led in Persimmon after the race

of faces which were to be seen at cock-fights and those other so-called sports which had survived the Regency. They were particularly to be seen at prize-fights, as at that famous match outside Farnborough in 1860 when Tom Sayers, the small and doughty English champion, was repeatedly knocked down by the huge American, John C. Heenan, in a drawn fight of thirty-seven rounds that lasted over two hours.

Ascot was rather more respectable. In an early issue of *The Illustrated London News* there appeared a picture of a fashionable picnic on Ascot Heath, the ladies sitting demurely under parasols in their carriages waited upon by gentlemen in tall black top hats, silk cravats, white waistcoats and tight-fitting frock coats. Male fashion was then in a transitional stage. The dandy of the 1830s, with his nipped waist, extravagantly flared coat, vivid necker-chief and tasselled walking stick was still sometimes to be encountered; but he was rather an old-fashioned figure. Men's clothes were becoming darker and more restrained. Sober black frock or tail coats, tubular trousers and top hats were *de rigueur* in London; and it was not until the late 1860s that

The final furlong at the Epsom races in 1860

74

lounge coats were worn by gentlemen in the country and that bowlers – the invention of the London hatter of that name – and straw hats began to be generally acceptable. Even in the 1890s the Prince of Wales still chose to wear a long coat and a top hat when riding in Rotten Row.

At the same time ladies' clothes became increasingly cumbersome. In 1837 a rich widow's young footman thought it 'quite disgusting . . . the way young ladies dress to attract the notice of the gentlemen. They are nearly naked to the waist, only just a little bit of dress hanging on the shoulder, the breasts are quite exposed except a little bit coming up to hide the nipples. Plenty of false hair and teeth and paint.' When this footman died over half a century later his modest eye had been gratified to see women clothe themselves in increasingly voluminous garments. By the middle of the century the crinoline was well established, remaining in fashion, disliked as it was, until 1870, when its gradual disappearance did not put an end to long, trailing skirts the hems of which had to be held up if the wearer wished to walk out. And even when out riding, ladies wore full skirts which almost touched the

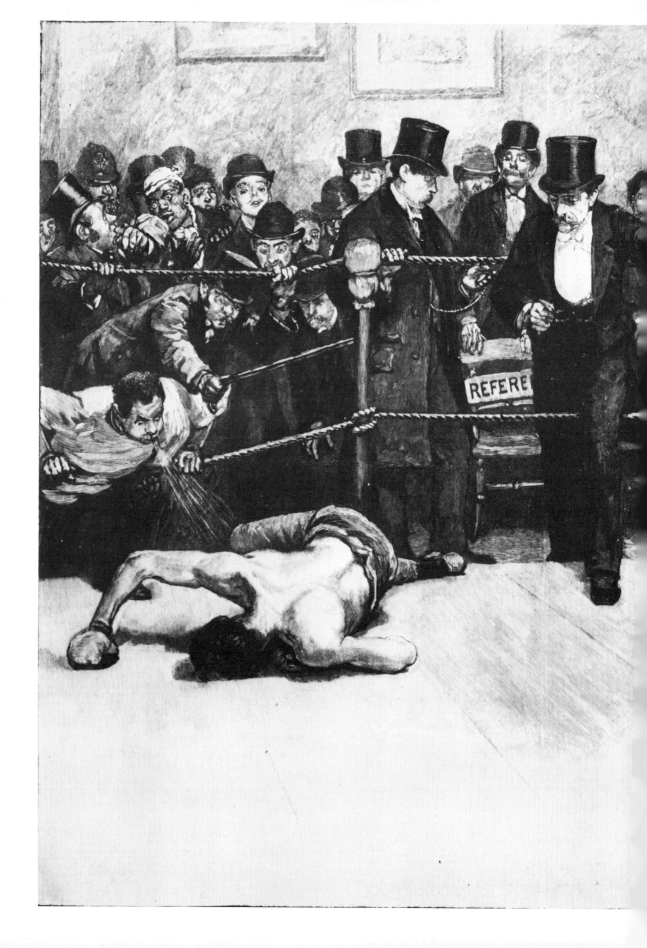

H.M.PAGET

ground as well as cloth trousers under thick, billowing petticoats and lace veils beneath top hats. The 'bloomer costume' of a short skirt with loose trousers gathered round the ankles, advocated by the American champion of women's rights, Mrs Amelia Jenks Bloomer, was considered more suited to socialist gatherings than ladies' drawing rooms. At least the bustle began to disappear towards the end of the century; but 'leg of mutton' sleeves did not; and it was not until 1890 that knickers began to be worn, at first in an apologetic way, being very long and wide and frilled at the edges, so that if seen at all, they would look like petticoats which they were intended to replace. It was not, in fact, for many years that they were to lead to the shorter skirt. At the turn of the century the nearest that women of fashion could approach towards casual wear was the separate blouse which, worn with a long skirt, had been first seen on the tennis court.

Throughout the century a lady's day would be punctuated by regular changes of costume. She might appear in her riding clothes at breakfast; but she would not do so at luncheon; nor would the clothes she wore at luncheon be suitable for tea; nor, of course, would the tea-gown be acceptable at dinner. Most of her days followed a set pattern of reading, needlework and writing letters, of drawing, perhaps, playing the piano or a game of croquet,

Ladies' fashions in 1847: on the left, a morning dress, on the right an evening dress, with the restrained use of a crinoline. Fashions were to become far more extravagant before the crinoline disappeared in the 1870s

Lady's fashion in 1897: a twopiece costume, with its severely nipped in waist and 'leg of mutton' sleeves

certainly of taking 'carriage exercise' and paying or receiving calls. In the evenings, when there were no guests to entertain, the needles would come out again and work would continue on all sorts of fancy-work and embroidery, decorative rather than useful; or the more enterprising ladies in the family would model fruit in wax or press flowers into albums or make pictures with shells. Perhaps the master of the house would read aloud to them or they would read to themselves. Sometimes they might look at photographs through stereoscopes or play a game of cribbage or halma, or sing a duet.

When the ladies had gone to bed, the men could put on their smoking caps and jackets and go to the gun-room or the billiard-room to smoke a cigar and drink a glass of brandy and water. In early Victorian England smoking was not as widespread as it later became; and there were many gentlemen who strongly objected to it, though few of them as strongly as Lord Melbourne who confessed that he always made a great row about it and if he smelled tobacco he swore 'perhaps for half an hour'. But Prince Albert smoked, so the Queen permitted the habit at Court, provided the gentlemen indulged it in the quarters allotted to them for the purpose, a rule which necessitated smokers taking a very long walk to the billiard-room at Windsor and, at Balmoral, walking across the open kitchen courtyard to a bare room near the servants' quarters. At Osborne House, however, the mansion which, with Prince Albert at his elbow, Thomas Cubitt designed for the royal family on the Isle of Wight, a special smoking room was built, the only room in the house with an 'A' by itself above the door instead of 'V and A'.

Osborne House was finished in 1848 and, for the rest of the century, not a year passed without the appearance of a new country house in one county or another. Several of them resembled Osborne, but most were built in other styles, usually Gothic.

Pictures of the interiors of many of these houses show how, as the century progressed, they became more and more cluttered with furniture and ornamentation. 'Wherever you can rest, there decorate,' Ruskin advised; and his advice was eagerly followed. Before the Great Exhibition of 1851 the taste of those who could afford to indulge any taste at all had been comparatively quiet and restrained, more in tune with the Georgian style which had preceded it than with the Victorian style which was to follow it when the Victorians first became fully aware of their own peculiar identity. After the Great Exhibition, where exhibits from all over the world, ornate, confusingly elaborate and voluptuously inventive, had been displayed in interiors overwhelming in their richness, the crowding had begun. Pieces of furniture, solid, comfortable, exotically decorated, multiplied in number and effusiveness; plain, rose-coloured silk-lined walls were overlaid with flock and patterned papers; back-to-back settees stood upon the thick pile of Brussels carpets. Behind the heavy outer curtains there appeared figured muslin inner curtains, edged and fringed. Porcelain figures, papier-mâché boxes and cut-glass bowls were set above white marble fireplaces beside the French clock, the candelabra and the gilt-framed chimney-glass. On a console table stood a model of a Swiss chalet brought back from Lausanne; on a purdonium a Benares tray purchased by a nephew on leave from the Poonah Horse; the embroidered handles of bell-pulls hung down beside the huge landscapes and seascapes, the prints and oleographs. Spring-upholstered chairs and sofas had banished earlier seats to the attic or the sale-room.

Before going for a spin Miss Jenny is very careful not to forget to put in her glove a few Poncelet's Pastilles.
She can avoid all risk of cold by keeping one in her mouth now and then when riding.

LISTEN! YOU WHO COUGH, TO GOOD ADVICE, AND TAKE PONCELET'S PASTILLES.

Poncelet's Pastilles are most Agreeable to the Taste. They Prevent and Cure Coughs, Colds, Bronchitis,
Hoarseness, Throat Irritation, &c., when all other remedies have failed. Their Action is Immediate.

1s. 1½d. PER BOX OF 100. OF ALL CHEMISTS.

Wholesale Depot: FASSETT & JOHNSON, 31 & 32, Snow Hill, London, E.C.

Towards the end of the century, under the influence of William Morris,
the more sophisticated Victorians began to send their unfashionable 'Exhibition art' to the sale-room also. William Morris, the archpriest of craftsmanship, whose designs for wallpaper, fabrics and carpets began a new chapter in
the history of interior decoration, urged people to have nothing in their
houses except those objects which they knew to be useful or believed to be
beautiful. It was an exhortation which the later Victorians did well to heed.

4 Pastimes and Pleasures

Holidays were rare and precious times. Until the middle of the century most men in full employment worked long hours six full days a week. Half-holidays were virtually unknown before factories in the textile industry were required to close by law on Saturday afternoons. Thereafter Saturday half-holidays spread to other trades; and the hours of full working days gradually shortened. In the late 1870s the phrase 'week-end' first came into use; and by the late 1880s the eight-hour day was becoming general throughout the country. It was beginning to be possible at last for working men to enjoy their leisure time instead of spending so much of it asleep in bed.

An Easter Monday excursion down the Thames to Greenwich and Blackheath in 1847

Hampstead Heath on a bank
holiday in 1872. The heath was
a favourite holiday haunt for
Londoners, and on fine days
over 10,000 people flocked there

According to Thomas Wright, a writer from a working-class background
in Manchester, the theatre was the most popular form of relaxation on a
Saturday evening. 'In order to get a place from which you can witness the
performance while seated,' Wright recorded, 'it is necessary to be at the
entrance at least half an hour before the doors open, and when they do open
you have to take part in a rush and struggle the fierceness of which can only
be credited by those who have taken part in such encounters.' It was also
necessary, Wright added, to take your own refreshments, those served in the
theatres being of a 'sickly and poisonous character . . . stale to the degree of
semi-putrefaction'. The refreshments served at music-halls were apparently
of rather better quality, 'but at the same time more than moderately dear,
while the waiters, who, in accordance with the usage of these establishments,
[had] to be "remembered" each time that they refilled your glass or brought
you the most trifling article, [haunted] you in an oppressive and vampirish
manner if you [ventured] to linger over your drink'. All things considered it
was not too much to say, 'notwithstanding the comparative low prices of
admission to them, music-halls [were] among the dearest places of amuse-
ment that a working-man [could] frequent'.

Opposite Scenes in the Royal
Victoria coffee palace and music
hall in 1881

Right Pantomime night as
depicted by Phiz in 1848; the
gallery, boxes and pit

The Royal Italian Opera House
at Covent Garden, which was
re-opened after a disastrous fire
in 1858

So they seem to have been in London where the first music-hall, Charles Morton's The Canterbury, was opened in 1851 and offered programmes of operatic arias, comic and patriotic songs and romantic ballads in surroundings of garish splendour. After The Canterbury came Weston's, later known as The Royal, in Holborn; then The Oxford, in Oxford Street, The Bedford, Evans', and innumerable other places, some fairly respectable, others certainly not; all noisy and exuberant and often attended as much for the pleasures of the bar and the barmaids as the performances given on the stage.

There were quite as many theatres in London as there were music-halls. There was The Princess's, in Oxford Street, where in the 1850s Charles Kean and his wife put on the plays of Shakespeare with great care for the historical accuracy of the settings and costumes; there was Sadler's Wells where Samuel Phelps gave his memorable performances as Falstaff; there was Covent Garden renamed The Royal Italian Opera House, where fashionable audiences listened to Verdi and Donizetti; there was The Haymarket where Benjamin Webster introduced audiences to the work of Charles Reade and Lord Lytton; there was Drury Lane where E. T. Smith provided a varied fare, combining drama with juggling and comedy with acrobats; and there was The Lyceum where Henry Irving began his distinguished reign. There were also, in the 1880s, three good theatres in the East End: The Standard in Norton Folgate, The Pavilion in the Mile End Road, and the Britannia in Hoxton – all homes of 'legitimate drama'. And in the outlying suburbs there were several theatres which presented everything from circuses to cabarets, from melodramas about Jack Sheppard to operettas about Ancient Rome. In addition, there were numerous private theatres where the seats were cheap and the parts were played by stage-struck amateurs who paid a fee for the privilege of doing so.

The most popular theatres of all were those on the south bank of the river which specialised in plays with highly melodramatic plots and much violent action – The Surrey, The Bower Saloon, The Pavilion, The City of London and The Coburg, better known as The Vic. Henry Mayhew described how when there was a play 'with a good murder in it' at The Vic, the crowds collected as early as three o'clock by the long zig-zag staircase which led to the paybox, youths standing on the broad wooden banisters about fifty feet from the ground and jumping on each other's backs to get into a better position in the queue.

Quite as popular as The Vic, though less plebeian and rowdy, was Astley's, a theatre in Westminster Bridge Road which presented an extraordinarily diverse fare including melodramas, circus clowns, acrobats, sword fights, elephants and dancing horses. Men earning less than £2 a week would cheerfully spend three or four evenings a week at Astley's, or at one or other of the smaller theatres where the productions might not be so spectacular but where the seats in the gallery would undoubtedly be as cheap. Even cheaper were the 'penny gaffs', the upper floors of shops which had been turned into places of entertainment where disreputable characters performed suggestive dances and sang obscene songs to the accompaniment of a rowdy band. 'Rude pictures of the performers . . . in their most "humorous" attitudes . . . are arranged outside,' Mayhew wrote, 'and at night time coloured lamps and transparencies are displayed to draw an audience.' Most of the customers were young girls and boys, some of them only eight years old, the boys lighting their pipes at the gas jets which spluttered on each side of the

Opposite Henry Irving as Shylock and *Overleaf* Ellen Terry as Portia in *The Merchant of Venice* at the Lyceum Theatre in 1880

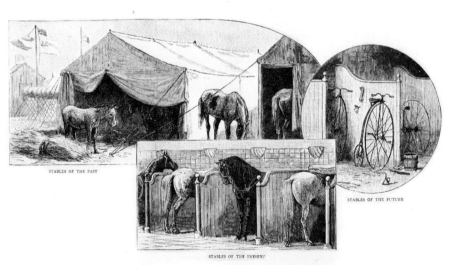

STABLES OF THE PAST

STABLES OF THE FUTURE

STABLES OF THE PRESENT

Right A circus on the move from
the summer edition of *The
Graphic*, 1888

91

makeshift proscenium, or tickling the girls who, 'dressed in showy cotton-velvet polkas with dowdy feathers in their crushed bonnets, stood laughing and joking with the lads in an unconcerned, impudent manner. Some of them, when tired of waiting, chose their partners and commenced dancing grotesquely, to the admiration of the lookers-on who expressed their approbation in obscene terms that, far from disgusting the poor little women, were received with compliments and acknowledged with smiles and coarse repartees.'

For those who preferred drinking to dancing there were public houses of infinite diversity and innumerable garish gin-shops behind whose bars of French-polished mahogany row upon row of barrels of gin were revealed in the light of glittering chandeliers. There were also numerous so-called coffee-shops where spirits as well as coffee were sold on the ground floor and in the cellars men bet on games of skittles or boxing matches.

'Englishmen will gamble on anything,' a foreign visitor remarked. And certainly betting was not limited to horse racing, greyhound racing and those animal sports like rat-killing which, though suppressed by law, still flourished more or less openly. Men bet on all manner of games, in fact, from football to cricket.

Various kinds of football had been played in England since time out of mind, the rules, where any were observed at all, being decided by local communities. The foundation of the Football Association in 1863, however, led to the gradual observance of standard rules which, by the time professional football was officially recognised by the Association in 1885, were accepted by all the leading clubs. The word soccer, which became respectable in 1891, was originally university slang; and was thereafter used rather derisively to distinguish 'association' football, which had become extremely popular with the working classes – particularly in the industrial north where huge crowds paid to watch the leading clubs – from the kind of football played with an oval ball. This game had originated at Rugby and in 1871 was governed by the Rugby Union, an organisation that banned professionalism within its member clubs, though in South Wales, Lancashire and on the Scottish Border rugger – another slang word from the universities – was played professionally and attracted large crowds of working-class supporters.

A football challenge cup match in March 1891 between Blackburn Rovers and Notts County

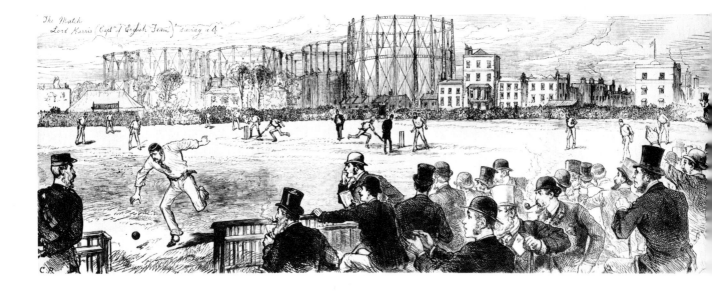

The Match
Lord Harris (Capt. of English Team) "during a 4"

Australia *versus* England at the Oval, 18 September 1880. W. G. Grace is shown keeping wicket for England

Cricket was also an old game which only slowly developed nationally recognised rules. At the beginning of the century it was still a rough game played on village greens with curved bats and balls thrown underarm. As organised ball games became an essential feature of the public-school ethos, however, cricket began to be bound by a code as strict as that governing a gentleman's conduct – the phrase, 'not quite cricket' already denoted ungentlemanly conduct before the nineteenth century was at an end. Gentlemen played cricket after leaving school either in amateur clubs like the I Zingari (founded in 1845) and the Gloucestershire county eleven (founded in 1870 by that national hero, Dr W. G. Grace and his two brothers), or in other county sides, like Nottinghamshire, which included both amateur and professional players.

Yet, popular as cricket was then becoming, it was not considered at the universities to be nearly as important as rowing. At Cambridge, indeed, in the year that the Grace brothers founded the Gloucestershire county eleven, only four Cambridge colleges had their own grounds; while the river was always full of crews, racing and practising, preparing for the regatta at Henley or for the great race against Oxford which was rowed for the first time in 1829 and which became an annual event in 1856.

Lawn tennis was then unknown. Unlike the older game which had been played in a court since the Middle Ages, the modern game was patented in 1874, under the name of 'Sphairistike', by Major Wingfield, whose original rules were altered three years later by the Wimbledon All England Croquet and Lawn Tennis Club. Golf, too, was a new game in England, although it had been played in Scotland for centuries and by Scotsmen living in England on Blackheath. The first English club, the Royal North Devon, was founded at Westward Ho in 1864 and the second, the Royal Liverpool Club, at Hoylake in 1869. Thereafter the number of players grew year by year, slowly at first – when most people seeing a man with a bag of clubs would suppose he was going to play polo, a game introduced from India in 1869 – but towards the end of the century very rapidly, women taking it up as well as men and after 1885 being admitted to the full courses from the shorter, separate links to which they had previously been banished.

94

Above Thames-side view of the
Oxford and Cambridge
university boat-race, 1889

Right Mixed doubles in the
South of England Lawn Tennis
tournament at Devonshire Park,
Eastbourne, 1888

Overleaf Rotten Row, Hyde
Park on a Sunday morning in
June 1885

As increasing numbers of people took to playing games, so did they travel more widely than they had ever done before. Every week-end family parties could be seen making their way to the nearest railway station, armed with guide-books and picnic hampers, perhaps to see a country house or a cathedral or one of those declining number of unspoiled beauty-spots which John Ruskin and his friend, Octavia Hill, were campaigning to preserve with the help, after its creation in 1895, of the National Trust. Or they might be going on an excursion organised by Thomas Cook who, encouraged by his success in booking a special train to convey people from Leicester to a temperance meeting at Loughborough, had begun to widen his activities with the Midland Railway in 1845. Not many could afford the 'Grand Circular Tour of the Continent' which Cook began to advertise in 1856, having successfully taken his customers from Leicester to Paris the year before. But increasing numbers went to the inland spas, to Buxton and Malvern, to Harrogate and to Matlock where Smedley's Hydropathic Establishment provided an ideal centre from which to take the beneficial waters of Derbyshire. And even greater numbers went to the sea-side – people from the north choosing Blackpool or Scarborough; Midlanders going to the coast of Wales; the genteel and retiring to Lyme Regis, Broadstairs and Folkestone; the fashionable to Eastbourne, Bognor and Cowes. The less well-to-do went to Margate, Ramsgate or Southend where they walked along the pier which no self-respecting resort could be without, or

The beach at Brighton in 1859, duly equipped with bathing huts

98

A medieval tournament held at the Cremorne pleasure gardens in Kings Road, Chelsea, 1863

congregated at the water's edge, peering out to sea through telescopes, knitting in the shade of umbrellas and parasols, reading newspapers and resisting the importunities of men selling ships in bottles and saucers of whelks; their children, as Frith depicted them on Ramsgate sands, running with bucket and spade between the Punch and Judy show and the nigger minstrels.

For those unable to leave the town there were the pleasures of the parks, the first of which, constructed in Birkenhead, was soon followed by that in Manchester, and then by those in other large provincial towns. In London there were not only parks but, until they degenerated into fun fairs or were sold to building speculators, there were also pleasure gardens. Vauxhall closed down in 1859; but there were many others offering food and drink in rustic bowers, music, dancing and fireworks and the peculiar specialities of the establishment. At the Hippodrome, Notting Hill, there was a miniature race-course; at the Red House, Battersea, there was pigeon shooting; the Flora Gardens, Camberwell, featured Lady Godiva in procession by torch-light; the Montpelier Tea Gardens, Walworth, once offered a cricket match between eleven one-legged and eleven one-armed pensioners of Greenwich Hospital. At Cremorne in King's Road, Chelsea, the most famous pleasure gardens of all, there were theatres and side-shows, shooting galleries, fortune-tellers and tightrope-walkers, circuses, water pageants and medieval tourna-ments. Unfortunately there were also numerous pickpockets and whores, rowdy boys and drunks; and Cremorne's reputation grew worse and worse until it closed down in 1877. The pleasure gardens of the Crystal Palace Company at Sydenham were much more respectable and offered musical concerts, exhibitions of painting and sculpture, tropical trees, architectural models and full-scale bronze dinosaurs.

In a society which was becoming ever more educated and intellectually curious there was a growing demand for such instructive displays. Crowds still flocked to the waxworks which Madame Tussaud transferred from Baker Street to Marylebone Road in 1884, paying particular attention then as now to the figures of the murderers. They still enjoyed the antics of Wombwell's Menagerie, and of the animals in the zoos at Walworth Manor House and in Regent's Park. They were still as capable as they had been in the eighteenth century of breaking out into the most violent riots, as they did in 1874 at Dukinfield where a pit disaster drew 100,000 morbid sightseers and where men from Manchester and Oldham fell upon each other with belts and knives. Yet over six million tickets were sold for the Great Exhibition, that demonstration of Britain's supreme achievements in manufacture and design which was given in the Crystal Palace – a 'marvel of Modern engineering' built by Joseph Paxton, whose conservatory at Chatsworth had been constructed in 1837 and whose design for the world's first prefabricated

A scene at the zoo on the first statute Bank Holiday, 19 August 1871. The crowd is being suitably entertained by the feeding of the lions

The opening of the new reptile house in the Zoological Society's Gardens in Regent's Park, 1883

public building originally appeared in *The Illustrated London News* in July 1851. And, as the daily crowds of 40,000 people walked round this great tribute to the virtues and rewards of hard work and patient industry; inspecting the machinery and inventions, the furniture and table glass; admiring the collapsible piano, Her Majesty's boudoir, and the knife with three hundred blades; gazing with awe upon Hiram Power's chaste Greek slave hiding her nakedness with manacled wrists, they were orderly and peaceful, impressed by man's progress and inspired to learn more about his prospects and his past.

In the second half of the century the people displayed an ever-growing interest in artistic and intellectual pursuits. Periodicals like the *Penny Magazine* and the *Family Economist*, which printed a number of educational articles in each issue, enjoyed a wide circulation, as did such publications as the YMCA series of *Lectures to Young Men*; while Samuel Smiles' self-improvement manual, *Self-Help*, sold a quarter of a million copies during the author's lifetime. Following the example of Andrew Carnegie, the Scottish-born American millionaire who founded several free libraries in his native land and in England, other philanthropists, including John Passmore

The construction of the Crystal
Palace in Hyde Park ready for
the Great Exhibition of 1851

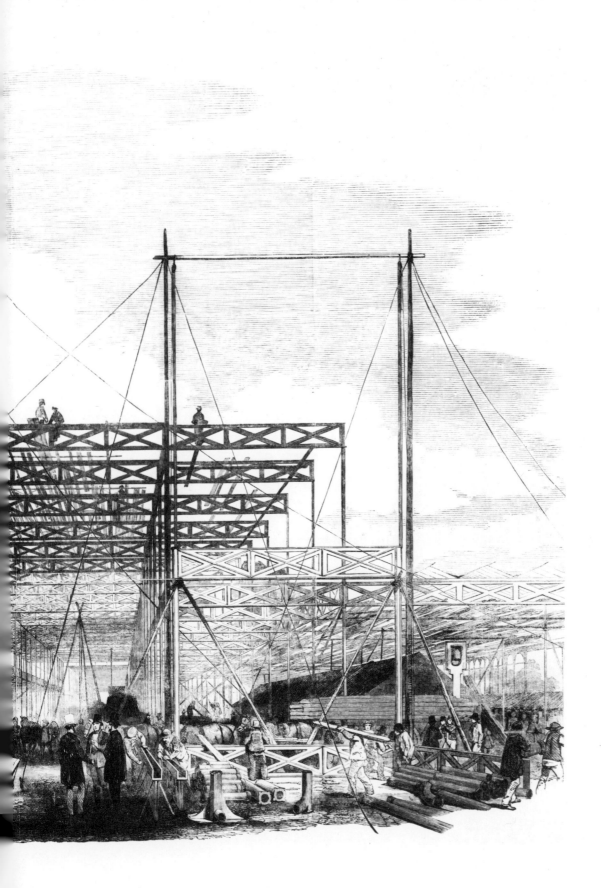

The main avenue at
the Great Exhibition

This page The five shilling and shilling days at the Great Exhibition – or, to quote *The Illustrated London News*: 'on one day, society – on the other the world'

Opposite A bedstead in the Renaissance style, exhibited at the Great Exhibition by Rogers and Dears

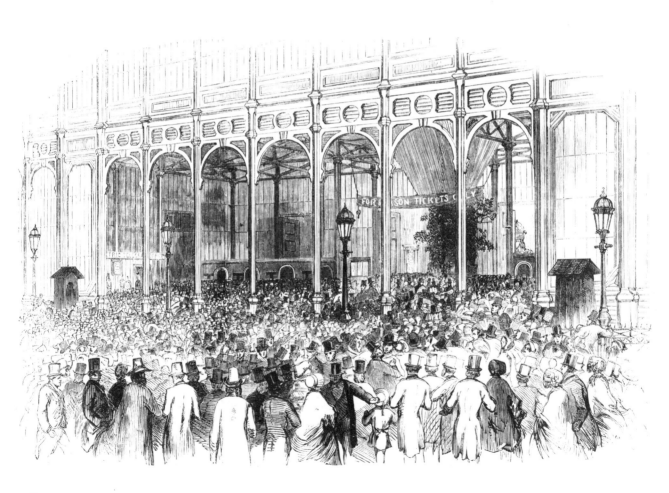

The first of a series of annual International Exhibitions of
Fine Arts and Industry was opened in May 1871 by the Prince of
Wales in Kensington, in a complex devoted to the perpetuation
of the memory of the Prince Consort. To the left of the picture
lies the Royal Albert Hall, and to the right the International
Exhibition Galleries

Edwards, former proprietor of the *Mechanics' Magazine* and the first halfpenny newspaper, the *Echo*, established lecture rooms, reading rooms and libraries all over the country. In 1892 the State came to the aid of the philanthropist with the Public Libraries Act, an improvement on an Act of 1850 which had applied only to boroughs of more than 10,000 inhabitants, had required the consent of two thirds of the ratepayers and had limited the library rate to 2d.

The number of Mechanics' Institutes was also increasing, the London

A concert of the Vocal Association, held at St James' Hall in April 1860

Mechanics' Institute of 1829 being followed by over six hundred others by 1860. And although many of the 600,000 members were clerks and shop-keepers, intent on self-improvement, rather than workers, there was at least no lack of institutions where the working man could find help and encouragement in the pursuit of any interest or course of education to which he could find the energy to devote his leisure time. 'The People's Palace,' wrote Charles Booth of one such institution, 'stands out conspicuously in East London as an attempt to improve and brighten the lives of the people. The Queen's Hall and the Library are fine buildings, the technical schools have suitable quarters, and there is a large swimming bath. The rest at present consists of "Exhibition Buildings" . . . The exhibitions . . . have been without end, very interesting and extremely well attended. The following societies and clubs are held in connection with this institution: Choral, boxing, dramatic, literary, cycling, cricket, football, harriers, chess and draughts, orchestral, Parliament, ramblers, photographic, sketching, shorthand and military band.'

At the end of the century there were also many more public art galleries and museums than there had been at the beginning. The National Portrait Gallery was opened in 1896; the Tate Gallery in 1897; the Wallace Collection in Manchester Square in 1900. In 1899 work had begun on the Victoria and Albert Museum which was built on land purchased with the profits of the Great Exhibition. Opposite it, the Natural History Museum, designed in Romanesque style by Alfred Waterhouse, was already complete. So was the Albert Hall, a huge circular red-brick building with a dome of glass and iron, reminiscent of an opera house at Dresden which Prince Albert had greatly admired. Not to be outdone by London, the big provincial cities were building art galleries and museums of their own, 'convinced at last,' as the chairman of the Great Northern Railway company put it on the occasion of the opening of Leeds Town Hall, 'that there were other matters well worth their attention besides manufacturing broadcloth for the purpose of making money'.

5 Nurseries and Schoolrooms

To the Victorians the concept of family life was held to be scarcely less than sacred. Indeed, Ralph Waldo Emerson thought that the family was the 'taproot' which enabled the English people to 'branch wide and high'. All their efforts were directed towards maintaining the 'independence and privacy of their homes'; nothing so much distinguished their character 'as the concentration of their household ties'. There were no songs so popular as those like *Home, Sweet Home* whose familiar music was greeted by cheers in music-halls and whose words, in poker-work or on samplers, were displayed on countless parlour walls. Despite a high rate of infant mortality which, in the middle of the century was about one in ten among the upper classes, one in six amongst the middle classes and one in four amongst the poor, families were often large, five or six children being commonplace, less than three unusual.

From all children the strictest submission to their parents' will was required as of right, obedience to higher authority being held as essential and unquestionable within the home as in the larger world outside it. 'Children, obey your parents in the Lord!' was an injunction as inviolable as 'Wives, obey your husbands!' And the husband who, except in the working classes, was alone responsible for the maintenance of the family's income and security, considered himself well justified in expecting such obedience.

Required to be seen, not heard, the children of well-to-do parents were, in fact, not often even seen. They lived in stuffy nursery quarters separate from the rest of the house, attended upon by nursemaids and schoolmaids, watched over by a governess, and ate those unappetising meals, with a high proportion of boiled vegetables and milk puddings, which were considered the only suitable fare for infant stomachs. Occasionally, they might be allowed down to the dining-room, when their parents had finished their meal, to have a small piece of fruit or a jelly. Sometimes the elder children were permitted to sit through a whole meal downstairs. But the smaller children, seeing their parents for only an hour or so each day and then expected to behave like miniature adults of an exceedingly quiet disposition, were left for most of their time in the care of their nurse, a servant as likely to resemble the creature in Charlotte M. Yonge's *The Daisy Chain*, who doped her small charge to death, as kind Clara Peggotty in *David Copperfield*. Drugs, medicines and restoratives were freely, not to say recklessly, administered. Wine was frequently prescribed by doctors; but it was left to the nurse to decide when the time had come to force down a reluctant throat a pill or powder, a dose of brimstone and treacle, castor oil, liquorice or a spoonful of the

Opposite and overleaf Governess and nursemaid with their respective charges, as seen by *The Sketch*

GOVERNESS : D—A—M—Dam, a thing to keep back water.
YOUNG PUPIL : When Papa says it, Mamma always cries.

NURSE : Now then, Master Georgie, you must come and have your face washed ; your grandfather's coming to tea.
GEORGIE : Yes ; but s'pose he don't come, what then ?

notorious Godfrey's cordial, that mixture of laudanum and syrup which, together with other similar products, could be purchased at any chemist's shop and which reduced children to varying states of stupefaction for hours on end. According to a report of 1844, 'great numbers of children perish, either suddenly from an overdose, or, as more commonly happens, slowly, painfully and insidiously'. And in those households where 'Godfrey's Cordial' or 'Daffy's Elixir' were banned from the medicine cupboard, much the same results were achieved by mixing liberal quantities of gin with the children's milk.

Boys from middle-class homes were dosed as unremittingly with brimstone and treacle and rhubarb and soda when they were sent away to board at a preparatory school. There they were also liable to be regularly flogged. At Temple Grove, East Sheen, it was customary to clench a Latin Grammar between the teeth to prevent screaming. The cruelty and squalor of most public schools were even more alarming. In early Victorian England there were only a few public schools which were recognised as such; but as the century progressed new establishments, claiming to offer a public school education, were founded at a rate which, fast as it was, was not fast enough to meet the demand of parents who were fully persuaded that no other sort of education was suitable for a gentleman. Marlborough, Rossall, Lancing, Cheltenham, and Radley were all founded in the 1840s; Wellington and Bradfield in the 1850s; Clifton, Haileybury and Malvern in the 1860s. The influence on these schools of such enlightened headmasters as Thomas Arnold of Rugby and Samuel Butler of Shrewsbury was considerable. But they remained for many boys dreaded institutions, memories of which haunted their later dreams; while for every civilised public school such as Uppingham, where Edward Thring transformed the small local grammar school, there were at least two others, like Worksop and Trent, where bullying was notorious. And, although the narrow curriculum of eighteenth-century Eton, which had formerly been a model for the other public schools, had been much widened, the classics were still its principal component, there being, as Sir George Young observed, hundreds of people who could teach them and hardly anyone who could teach anything else. 'If you want science,' Faraday told a Royal Commission, 'you must begin by creating science teachers.'

'The Greek and Latin grammars, and portions of the easier classic authors – cricket – boating – the price of tarts, and of wine by the bottle, and perhaps the names of the head and assistant masters of the school: these are,' so it was alleged in 1850, 'the particulars of the [public schoolboy's] vast sum of knowledge.' Even at Rugby, long after Arnold's time, over three quarters of the lessons were devoted to the classics.

By no means all those parents who could afford it sent their sons to a public school. The second Earl Grey did not; nor did Disraeli's father; Ruskin was educated by his mother; Sir Richard Burton was given no formal education at all. Tennyson did not go to a public school; nor did Lord Macaulay; nor the poet, Coventry Patmore; nor the scientist, Lord Armstrong. In Gladstone's fourth cabinet of seventeen members, only eight were educated at public schools – four at Eton, two at Harrow, one at Cheltenham and one at Rugby. Four were educated privately; two at Glasgow High School; one at the City of London School; one at St Saviour's Grammar School, Southwark; and one at a Board School in Leicester.

Many a country squire considered it quite sufficient to send his son to a nearby grammar school where – though he would continue to speak in the local dialect as his ancestors had done for generations – he would be likely to get quite as good an education as he might have received at a public school. Edward Hamley, the future general, for instance, whose family had been settled in Cornwall since the conquest, was sent to Bodmin Grammar School. There were not enough good grammar schools, though; and several of the best had been established centuries before in small towns now inaccessibly remote. And so the number of public schools continued to grow as the social ambitions of the middle classes increased, as the proliferation of railways made it easier to send a boy away to board, and as it became increasingly necessary to pass examinations to enter the professions, the Civil Service and even, if you were not rich or of distinguished birth, to go to Oxford and Cambridge.

These two universities long held their monopoly, resisting change within their own institutions as strongly as competition from without. For many undergraduates they were no more than resorts of pleasure or, as a Royal Commission reported of Oxford in 1852, places of 'sensual vice, gambling . . .

Opposite The new buildings erected by the City of London School on the Thames Embankment near Blackfriars Bridge in 1882

extravagant expenditure . . . and driving, riding and hunting'. Throughout the 1860s noblemen still sported a golden tassel on their mortar-boards to denote their special status; and it was not until 1871 that Fellows were allowed to marry and that the stranglehold of the Anglican Church, which had been firmly opposed to the abolition of religious tests, was finally broken. Very slowly did other universities – London and Durham leading the way – achieve any comparable recognition as seats of learning, qualified to award degrees; and never were they accorded the same social prestige.

Once the dam had been broken, however, reforms swept along fast. After the middle of the century science laboratories began to appear at Oxford, although headmasters, most of them clergymen, had become wary of the subject as an inducement to paganism after the appearance in 1859 of Charles Darwin's *Origin of Species*. In 1871 Cambridge was presented with the Cavendish Laboratory by the Duke of Devonshire, Chancellor of the University. An undenominational college was founded at Manchester; which, combined with other colleges founded at Liverpool and Leeds, became Victoria University in 1884; several medical colleges were opened in the provincial towns of the north and Midlands, including Leeds and Birmingham. Scottish universities, much cheaper than English ones, continued to prosper. They also provided the kind of technical education which in England, despite the efforts of the Royal Institution and the Royal School of Mines and Science, was much neglected. For instance, in Leeds, which already had a population of a quarter of a million in 1867, the single technical instructor was a teacher who was paid £11 a year to give lessons on chemistry in a cellar. Conscious of this neglect, philanthropic manufacturers such as Sir Josiah Mason urged that 'all classes [should be] given the means of

carrying on their scientific studies as completely and thoroughly as . . . in the
great science schools of the Continent'. With this aim in view Mason
University College, later to obtain a charter as Birmingham University, was
founded in 1872. Other similar university colleges soon followed: in 1893
the three Welsh colleges, Aberystwyth, Cardiff and Bangor, were formed
into the University of Wales: and even women, who had hitherto been
regarded as unsuitable for a classical let alone a mathematical education,
were admitted to their lectures.

Before 1840 the education of those few girls who were given any formal
instruction at all had been left to governesses and to teachers in schools where
deportment was regarded as far more important than mere learning and
where the only form of exercise permitted the girls was a sedate walk in a
'crocodile'. In 1847, however, in the face of much criticism and ridicule,
Queen's College, London, was founded for young ladies, one of whom,
Dorothea Beale, became principal of Cheltenham Ladies' College; and
another, Frances Mary Buss, established the North London Collegiate
School for Ladies which, after the opposition of various parents had been
overcome, admitted the children of tradesmen. The success of this school
paved the way for various other worthy establishments, notably in 1874,
Manchester High School for Girls.

By then women undergraduates had at last appeared at Cambridge.
Already admitted to London and Victoria Universities, they had arrived at
Newnham College at Cambridge in 1871. The next year Girton College,
founded at Hitchin in 1869, moved to Cambridge. And in 1879 Lady

Margaret Hall and Somerville were opened as the first Oxford women's colleges. Women were not yet admitted to full equality with men; but their foothold in the universities was now secure.

To the great mass of the people, however, education was still but a fitful process. In the 1850s there were various types of school available for working-class children, few of them the responsibility of the State. For the youngest there were dame schools whose main purpose was to keep the children confined and quiet; there were private day schools where the quality of the teaching was reflected in the low fees – less than sixpence a week – which were demanded and which, even so, many parents could not afford to pay; there were factory schools which were ill-equipped, ill-staffed and ill-

A dame school in 1856

attended; there were Sunday schools for the respectable poor; and there were Ragged schools for the rough and dirty urchins like those who were sent to that established by the social reformer, Quintin Hogg, wearing nothing other than their mothers' threadbare shawls. For the sons of farmers there were 'county schools' whose fees few farmers paid without grumbling about the fancy ideas their lads might acquire. And for boys who got or might get into trouble there were Boys' Homes where attempts were made to feed, clothe and educate the uneasy incumbents for £15 each a year. There were also schools run by various religious groups and charities which were better than most but whose places were limited. And there were, of course, those dreadful schools which had been established in Yorkshire where unwanted children were boarded and supposedly educated with 'no extras' and 'no vacations' for twenty guineas a year, as at Bowes Academy which Dickens indicted as Dotheboys Hall in *Nicholas Nickleby*.

There was, indeed, no lack of variety in schools – nor, it may be added, in the quality of teachers, over seven hundred of whom in 1851 could not even sign their names. The problem was to get the children to attend their lessons. In 1851 less than half the children of school age in England attended any school at all; and of those that did very few remained after the age of eleven. Ten years later the situation began to improve as children were gradually prevented from working in certain industries and as their parents became less dependent upon their offsprings' earnings. At the same time the government started to exert a long-delayed authority: in 1870 it was at last enacted that there should be a school within reach of every child; and ten years later, after many new schools had been built, attendance was made

The work room of the ragged school in Brook Street, 1853

124

compulsory and crowds of children running wild in the streets were no longer a common sight. In 1891 school fees for elementary education were abolished; and the school leaving age gradually rose – to eleven in 1893, to twelve in 1899 and to fourteen in 1900.

The education provided at many of the schools run by the recently created local School Boards was, however, far from as satisfactory as such advocates of a liberal education as T. H. Huxley would have liked. Many pupils arrived at school in a condition far from conducive to acquiring any education at all. 'Puny, pale-faced, scantily clad and badly shod', 50,000 children were believed to go to school in want of food as late as 1889. Nevertheless, the long struggle against illiteracy was gradually won. In 1850 scarcely more than half the population of England could sign their names; and, in the Midlands, almost three quarters of those who had been to school might just as well have stayed away, for they were still, to all intents and purposes, illiterate. In 1867 a survey revealed that half the working population of Manchester could still not read; and other surveys suggested that the literacy rate in similar towns was much the same, except in Scotland where the number of children at secondary school and of students at university was far higher than in England and where nearly every one could read and write. By 1880, however, the rate of illiteracy in England had fallen to twenty per cent; and by 1900 only about three per cent of the population could not sign their names in the marriage register.

Yet in the poorest districts truancy from school was still endemic. 'Children are given food in a handkerchief and live in the street, coming or not coming to school at will,' a schoolmaster complained in the 1890s. 'Sometimes they are lost for a week or two, living meanwhile by begging or pilfering. It is useless to speak to the parents.' Thousands of others did not go to school because they went to work. Indeed, the problem of the working child was one of the most intractable of all the problems that faced the Victorian reformer.

6 The Oppressed

For most of the nineteenth century children could be seen in every city street selling matches and newspapers, sweeping crossings, holding horses, running errands, fetching jugs of beer from public houses, cleaning shoes. In the earlier decades there were thousands more, many of them under five years old, employed by their parents at home or in sweating-shops in the clothing, lace-making and straw-plaiting trades, pinned to their mothers' knees to keep them at work and being slapped on the head to keep them awake.

Left and opposite Familiar figures from the Victorian streets: the crossing-sweep and a little flower-seller in Trafalgar Square

127

Others were employed in the houses of neighbours looking after babies – though scarcely more than babies themselves – and doing what little housework was considered necessary. In the country they were paid to work in agricultural gangs or to scare crows with rattles or to tend sheep. Many were employed in the ribbon trade, three hundred of them in Coventry, turning handlooms. 'The incessant whirl has so bad an effect on the head and stomach,' it was reported at the time, 'that the little turners often suffer in the brain and spinal cord, and some have died of it. In one scutching mill . . . six fatal cases and sixty mutilations have occurred in four years . . . There is no doubt that a great deal of quiet murder, perfectly appalling when attention is called to it, is continually going on among the juvenile population.'

Conditions were quite as bad for children employed in the paper staining, chain-making and cartridge-making trades; and they were even worse in the pottery trade where boys acted as mould-runners in temperatures of up to 120 degrees, hurrying with the plate-maker's full mould to the stove-room and then rushing back with an empty one.

Protection of children from exploitation came very slowly. The Mines and Collieries Act of 1842 put an end to very young boys and girls working in mines where for generations they had been employed, from the age of six, in pushing and dragging coal carts, crawling on hands and knees in cold,

Children were often employed by their parents at home or in sweating-shops. This picture shows children and adults making matchboxes in a house in Bow in 1871. The going rate at that time was 2½d the gross, and the worker had to find his own paste and twine

damp, dark tunnels, many of them never seeing the light of day for weeks on end during the winter season. But it was not until 1860 that the starting age for underground work was raised from ten to twelve. And, although children under nine could no longer be legally employed in textile factories by that time, it was not until a whole series of acts were passed later on in the 1860s that young children were kept out of other, often more unpleasant, factories and workshops. Even then there were many specific exemptions and illegal evasions; and so there continued to be long after 1870 when it was decided at last that all children under the age of ten should go to school.

The parents of child workers often argued that the younger children in the family would go hungry were it not for the few extra shillings that their elder brothers and sisters could bring home. And there was justice in the claim. Most Victorians, in fact, were poor, if not by the standards of other Europeans of their day, certainly by those of modern society. The average real income per head of the population in 1855 was £20 a year compared with £78 a hundred years later; and in bad years tens of thousands of men, women and children were close to starvation. The pattern of poverty was constantly changing: a family in comfortable circumstances one year might find themselves destitute the next; the relatively good years after the 'Hungry Forties' – when unemployment was at its peak, when industry seemed on the verge of collapse and food prices rose higher and higher – were followed by

The Earl of Shaftesbury visiting a coal mine in the Black Country during his investigation of the employment of children in collieries and mines. As a result of his report, the 1842 Act stopped children under the age of ten working below ground

another depression in the 1870s. Yet even in the better years poverty was, for many, inescapable; and throughout the 1850s and 1860s, over a quarter of the population still lived in painful indigence. Gladstone spoke of the gradual, ineluctable improvement of the masses; but as late as 1885 a survey conducted by the *Pall Mall Gazette* concluded that one in four people in London lived in abject poverty.

It was such conclusions as these that induced Charles Booth to conduct an exact and lengthy enquiry of his own which revealed an appalling extent of hardship and squalor amongst the poor. Some of his contemporaries could not believe that the facts set down by Booth and his team of investigators were as bad as they stated them to be. Similarly Alderman Sir Peter Laurie declined to believe that there was, or ever had been, such a filthy, evil and disturbing place as Jacob's Island in Southwark, although Dickens' description of it in *Oliver Twist* was almost discreet in comparison with the factual account of it given by Henry Mayhew in that series of articles from which developed *London Labour and the London Poor*. It was distressing enough to be assured by Booth that in eighty-five per cent of cases the causes of poverty were not 'idleness, drunkenness or thriftlessness' as had so often been propounded in the past, but lack of work, low pay, sickness or a large family. It was even worse to discover that of the six categories into which Booth divided the labouring classes only two came 'above the line of poverty'. Apart from

The registration of unemployed at Chelsea in 1887. This office was organised on a voluntary basis; unemployment exchanges were not controlled by the government until after 1900

Distribution of soup to the
poverty-stricken in Stranger's
Home, Limehouse in 1868

the 'occasional labourers, loafers and semi-criminals', there were countless
numbers of men and women working as dockers, building labourers or in the
various so-called sweated trades who did not, 'on the average, get as much as
three days' work a week'. Some of these irregularly employed men were
coal-backers who could 'very quickly earn 15s. or 20s.', though at 'the cost
of great exhaustion' and at the risk of rendering themselves unfit for any
further work by the age of forty. But there were others, such as cabinet-
makers, who, working in a sweat-shop, would turn out a dozen what-nots in
a day and a half for which he would be given no more than 3s.

In sweat-shops, where carpenters, tailors and chain-makers worked
inordinately long hours, the conditions were as horrifying as the wages were
precarious. A Parliamentary Committee, appointed to report on the sweating
system in 1890, heard of a 'double room, perhaps nine by fifteen feet, in
which a man, his wife and six children slept and in which same room ten
men were usually employed, so that at night eighteen persons would be in
that one room . . . with . . . three or four gas jets flaring, a coke fire burning
in the wretched fireplace, sinks untrapped, closets without water and
altogether the sanitary condition abominable'. In another tailoring work-
shop 'the water-closet is in the shop itself; the females sit within three feet of
it . . . There is great want of decency, and it is easy to imagine what follows
on such contamination. . . . Three mechanics are at work; there is one fireplace and eight or nine gas jets, also a sky-light, which, when broken, exposes

A military tailor with his family in his home in Bethnal Green in 1863. The poverty of the surroundings and the overcrowded conditions are all too plain

the workers to the rain. On complaints being made, the sweater says, "If you can't work go home." . . . In nine cases out of ten the windows are broken and filled up with canvas; ventilation is impossible, and light insufficient. [A witness] said that the poor people, who formerly occupied two or three rooms, are now, for the most part, driven to occupy one room. There they live by day and night, and there is to be found all the trade refuse in the room, creating an immense danger not only to themselves but to their neighbours. "You can tell when work is being done on the Sabbath by the blinds being drawn" . . . As the workshops are described by witnesses to be miserable; so is the food stated to be of the poorest description. "I am almost ashamed to say what my food is." Ordinary diet, a cup of tea and a bit of fish. "Meat I do not expect; I might get meat once in six months." '

The work was as uncertain as the wages were meagre and irregular. 'Sometimes,' one workman said, 'we have nothing to do for weeks and weeks, but have to go idle.' Then there would be a rush of work and he would be constantly employed from six o'clock in the morning until midnight. Other witnesses worked for twenty-two hours at a stretch; one had worked for forty. They had 'an hour for dinner, no tea time'. Most of them were paid by the piece – a woman might get $7\frac{1}{2}$d. for a coat 'and by working fifteen hours she could make four such in the day, earning 2s. 6d.; but out of this she had to pay 3d. for getting the button-holes worked, and 4d. for trimmings'. Men made slightly more than women, but frequently had to be content with 2s. 6d. a day when they were paid at all.

Although women and children were prevented from working underground, they were still employed by mine workers for surface work and in factories where their conditions were little better than they had been in the pits. Life in factories in the cotton industry, which in the middle years of the century employed almost 200,000 women and about 15,000 children under thirteen, was relatively tolerable. But in Bryant and May's match factory, for instance, conditions were not merely unpleasant but dangerous; yet it was not until the women were persuaded to strike in 1888 that the public heard of their sufferings and of 'phossy jaw', a kind of necrosis caused by the phosphorus with which they had to tip the sticks. And there were many other factories as bad as, or even worse than, Bryant and May's.

Unpleasant as life was in these factories, though, it could be quite as disagreeable and almost certainly less rewarding for women who had to work at home or in other people's homes: pipe makers, for example, had to make an immense number of pipes to earn a bare subsistence; while most of their business was done with publicans whose practice it was to demand that the women should spend 3d. in drink for every shilling's worth of pipes that they bought. Women were obliged to do such work since obtaining employment at all in many areas was difficult; and even a few pence could make a great deal of difference to the family budget. There were sewing jobs for some, washing work for others, a few vacancies in shops, though even in milliners' and drapers' shops male employees were still far more common as late as the 1880s; and in tobacconists' and confectioners' the girls had a reputation for

Pit-brow women in Lancashire in 1887. Legislation had prevented women and children working underground, but these women were employed to sift the smaller coal in the mound of earth and shale at the mouth of the pit

Above Women compositors working at the printing office of the Victoria Press in Great Coram Street in London

Opposite The 1833 Factory Act had made a humble start in limiting the hours worked by women and children in mills and factories. It also – and this was a very significant step – had appointed for the first time factory inspectors to enforce the legislation. In this illustration a government inspector is checking that the children are getting the schooling required by the law, and that their daily working hours are duly limited

providing their customers with other services in their spare time. Nurses, like shop assistants, were mostly male: in the 1840s, in fact, before Florence Nightingale went to train in Germany, only about five in a thousand hospital nurses were women; and by the 1880s the number of female nurses had increased by less than fifty per cent. So, inevitably, most women who had to find work, and had neither the talent nor the training to do anything else, became domestic servants and were then as frequently exploited by their employers as they were elsewhere in a society where unskilled labour was cheap because it was both plentiful and unorganised.

For those women whose social position rendered them unsuitable for manual work or domestic service, there were even less opportunities. Some became teachers or governesses – over 125,000 by 1881 – others became clerks or secretaries, though not many until the typewriter came into general use and contributed to a sudden and enormous increase in the number of women working in offices – from only 7,000 in 1881 to 90,000 twenty years later. Towards the end of the century a few – a very few – women entered the professions whose doors had hitherto been firmly closed against them and were unlocked in the face of much opposition and ridicule. Elizabeth Blackwell succeeded in getting her name placed on the Medical Register

with an American degree in 1858 and Elizabeth Garrett Anderson was admitted to the Register in 1865 with a Licence from the Society of Apothecaries. But it was not until 1876, two years after the establishment of the London School of Medicine for Women, that an Act was passed 'removing the Restrictions on the Granting of Qualifications on the Ground of Sex'. And even then the existence of female doctors was much regretted by the medical profession as a whole. 'Certain *persons* have succeeded in passing the examinations thrown open to them,' the *Lancet* loftily informed its readers in June 1882, 'and others may do the same, but the world and the good sense of the sex will no more permanently tolerate the unseemly invasion of an unsuitable province of labour than women, as a class, will ultimately show themselves fitted for the discharge of the duties they have rashly, and, as we believe, indecorously undertaken.'

The *Lancet*'s views were not in the least exceptional. Women were, as T. H. Huxley put it, brought up to be 'either drudges or toys beneath man,

Above Women employed as match-makers at Bryant & May's factory in Bow, 1871. The workers were expected to tip the matches with phosphorus, and this often caused a very unpleasant condition known as 'phossy jaw'. In 1888 the Bryant & May match-girls went out on strike against these dangerous conditions and won their case

Opposite The Bar of the Divorce Court at Westminster in 1870

or a sort of angel above him'. They were – it was not their fault – less intelligent than men; they did not share – unless they were depraved – men's sexual appetites; God had not intended them to have the same rights as men, the same privileges or the same responsibilities. Their proper place was in the home; and there most of them stayed waiting for a husband.

Yet marriage substituted one master for another. A married woman's possessions automatically became those of her husband until the law was changed between 1870 and 1883. Up till 1852 a wife had no right in common law to leave an intolerable husband who could force her to come back to him if she had the courage to run away; and women had to wait until 1891 before earlier authority was set aside by the Court of Appeal which ruled that a husband could not legally detain his wife in his house against her will. Divorce was obtainable only by Act of Parliament before 1857; and even after that, while a husband could divorce his wife for adultery, she had to prove not only that her husband was an adulterer, but also that he was guilty of some additional offence such as desertion, rape, incest or sodomy. Were she prepared to go through the ordeal of submitting herself to examination on these points and even if she won her case, she would find herself ostracised from many houses. Only within the last few years of her life did Queen Victoria allow even the innocent party in a divorce suit to appear at Court.

A woman who was separated from her husband was, for the first time in 1839, allowed custody of their children under seven; but it was not until 1873 that the age limit was raised to sixteen. For most of the Victorian age, indeed, women had as few rights and as little freedom as the 'doll in the doll's house' which Bella Rokesmith complains of being in *Our Mutual Friend* or Sally Brass' downtrodden maid in *The Old Curiosity Shop* who is 'ignorant of the taste of beer, unacquainted with her own name (which is less remarkable) and [takes] a limited view of life through the keyholes of doors'.

7 Criminals and Reformers

In 1867, according to 'reliable police statistics', there were in London no less than 100,000 persons who lived by plunder and did not know where their day's food was to come from when they got up in the morning. There were pickpockets and shop-lifters, housebreakers and burglars, horse-stealers and footpads; there were sneaksmen who dipped their nimble fingers into shop tills and carriage windows, bug-hunters who specialised in robbing drunks, shofulmen who were expert in passing counterfeit money. There were also thousands of beggars representing themselves as ship-wrecked sailors or crippled miners, displaying their own or their children's twisted limbs and open sores. Whole quarters of the city were occupied by people living wholly or partly on the proceeds of crime. In Lambeth and Southwark, Spitalfields and Seven Dials, there were mazes of courts and rookeries protected by ferocious guard dogs from the attentions of strangers or authority and riddled with manholes and tunnels, concealed passages and hidden exits, so that a criminal in danger of arrest could soon escape from his pursuers. In these and other areas equally insalubrious, tens of thousands of people slept in rotting, verminous tenements or in filthy lodging-houses where the charge was twopence a night for a bundle of rags on a bunk. For a penny reduction in the fee, an inmate could sleep on the floor of the kitchen; and many did so, women as well as men, girls as well as boys, most of them having taken the precaution of getting drunk if they could afford it, for otherwise there was no sleep to be had. 'There was very wicked carryings-on,' a young girl told Henry Mayhew. 'We lay packed on a full night, a dozen boys and girls all mixed. I can't go into all the particulars . . .'

By day these boys might work for some such ogre as the celebrated Taff Hughes – a far more terrifying figure than Dickens' Fagin – who would turn in fury on any little thief who came back empty-handed and flog him with the strap that held on his wooden leg. The girls, if not prostitutes already, would as likely as not soon become so, providing new diversions for the brothels of Windmill Street where, as a police superintendent recorded, elderly gentlemen could be found in every room with two children in each bed.

There were an estimated 80,000 professional prostitutes in London in the 1860s, as well as uncounted thousands of amateurs known as 'dolly mops'. Many of the professional girls were under fifteen; and more than half worked in brothels of which there were about three thousand in all, the most squalid being down by the Docks where, in certain courts, every room in

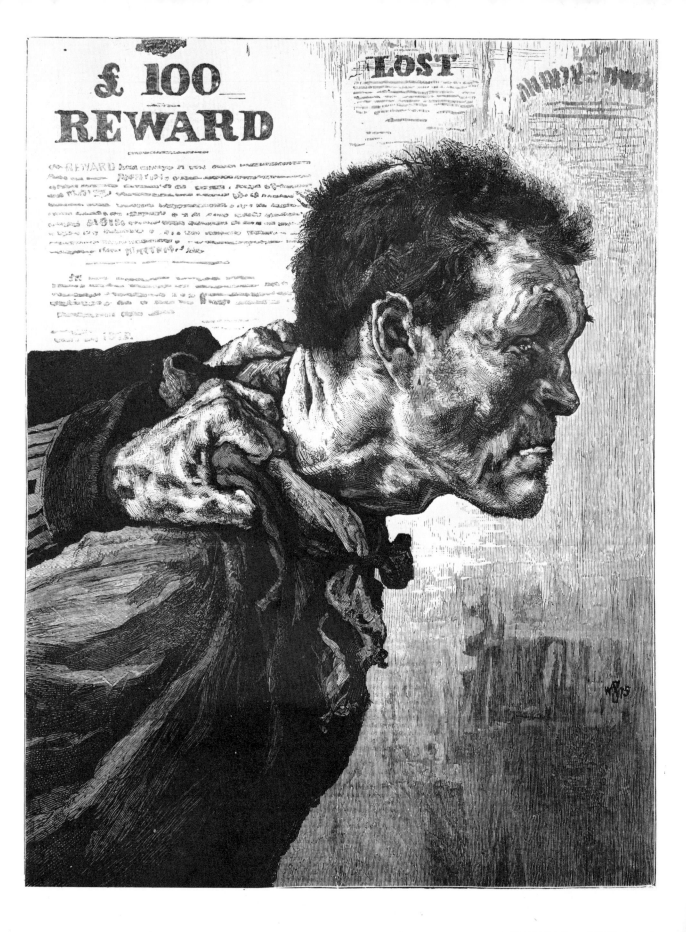

every house was given over to prostitution. But it was not only in the East End that girls could be found ready to offer themselves for the price of a glass or two of gin. The Haymarket, a contemporary writer recorded, was 'absolutely hideous at night with its sparring snobs, and flashing satins, and sporting gents, and painted cheeks, and bawdy-sparkling eyes, and bad tobacco and hoarse horse laughs and loud indecency'. Nor was London exceptional. Every large town had its brothels and its whores, its betting clubs where prostitutes sat waiting for customers on the floor beneath the gaming-tables, its seedy music-halls where girls paraded up and down the bar singing the choruses of the obscene songs and providing a running commentary on the *poses plastiques*.

The Illustrated London News was less concerned with such places than with the measures that were being taken to reform their *habitués* and to bring the criminal to justice. The paid police force, created in London by Robert Peel's Metropolitan Police Act, had been slow to spread to the provinces where crime increased at a fearful rate as predators, driven from London by the growing efficiency of its police, transferred their activities to towns in which old-fashioned methods of crime detection still prevailed. Following the recommendations of a Royal Commission, an Act was passed permitting counties to raise and equip paid police forces; and those counties that took advantage of the Act soon had cause to be thankful that they had done so. Yet in 1853 there were still twenty-two counties which continued to rely on an amateur force, with disastrous results, particularly for the poorer inhabitants who could not afford the payments the local constables traditionally demanded. So in 1856 another Police Act was passed making it obligatory for all counties to raise and maintain a constabulary. Its beneficial effects were soon apparent; serious crimes against property fell steeply; so did crimes of violence which, Edwin Chadwick had estimated in the late 1830s, cost 11,000 lives every year. An efficient professional police force was at last recognised to be an important means of preventing crime.

If Britain's new police helped to prevent crime, however, the country's new prisons did nothing for the reformation of the habitual criminal. In earlier years the State had found a convenient method of ridding itself of unwanted miscreants by transporting them to the colonies, originally to America before the Revolutionary War suddenly forced the government to look for other means of disposing of those criminals who were allowed to escape hanging, and then to Australia until the respectable settlers refused to allow their continent to be used as a dumping-ground any longer. Tasmania, 'swamped with the criminal classes from England' and deserted by its free colonists, refused to accept any more convicts in 1852. A request to Queensland to take them in was promptly met by an enquiry as to whether there was not some part of Britain which might prove a suitable penal settlement for Queensland's criminals. For a time Western Australia was more obliging; but the last convict ship to sail there left England in 1867.

By this time earnest efforts had been made to reform the British penal system on the lines of those American institutions which, in order to prevent prisoners corrupting each other, kept them in separate cells and forbade them to talk. A vast prison building programme had therefore been undertaken in order to make it possible to run British prisons on American lines. No less than fifty-five prisons were constructed in the 1840s, many of them, like Reading Prison to which Oscar Wilde was committed in 1895, combining

'with the castellated . . . a collegiate appearance'. The first was Pentonville which had 520 cells, each thirteen feet long and seven feet broad, with a stool, a table, and a hammock. On reception all the new prisoners were perfunctorily inspected by the medical officer, then lectured by the Governor about the rules and punishments, then preached at by the Chaplain, then stripped and made to stand before an officer 'in a perfect state of nudity while he examined with disgusting particularity every part of their persons'. Finally they were issued with a mask of brown cloth so that they would be unrecognisable when allowed out of their cells, 'the eyes alone appearing through the two holes cut in the front'. In the prison chapel, which he was required to attend daily, each prisoner had his own pigeon-hole of a pew so that, although his head was visible to the warders on duty, he was hidden from the view of his neighbours.

Work in most prisons began at six o'clock in the morning and was largely devoted to tasks which were usually pointless, sometimes degrading, often exhausting and always monotonous. The convicts were placed in a tread-wheel, a big iron frame of steps around a revolving cylinder, and required to trudge up the steps in separate compartments for six hours a day. Or they were made to turn a crank in a box of gravel, completing 10,000 revolutions before their labour was considered done. Or they were required to pick pieces of old rope to pieces though the use of iron in the building of ships had rendered the resultant oakum virtually unsaleable. 'The work of picking oakum is rather painful,' *The Illustrated London News* reported of the work undertaken in the House of Correction in Clerkenwell in 1874, 'but becomes

142

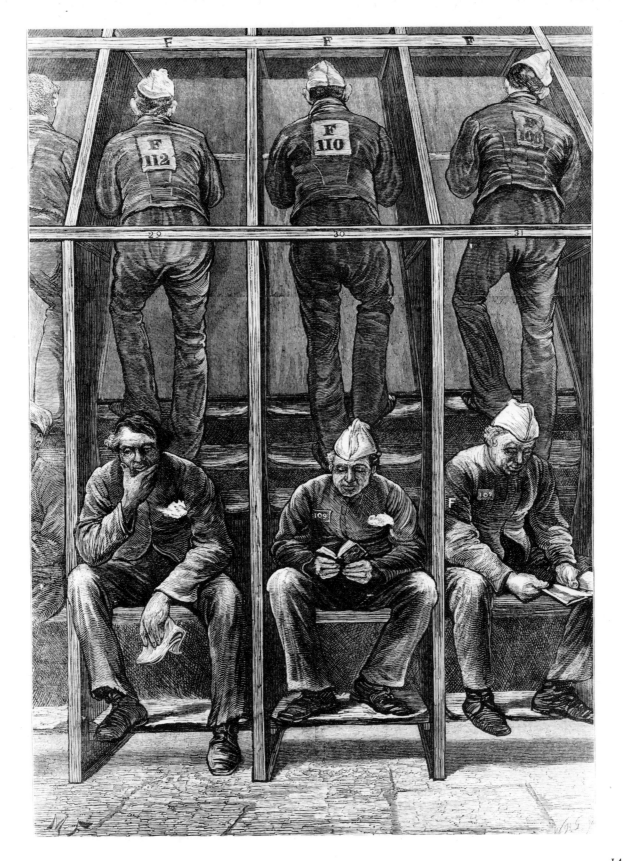

143

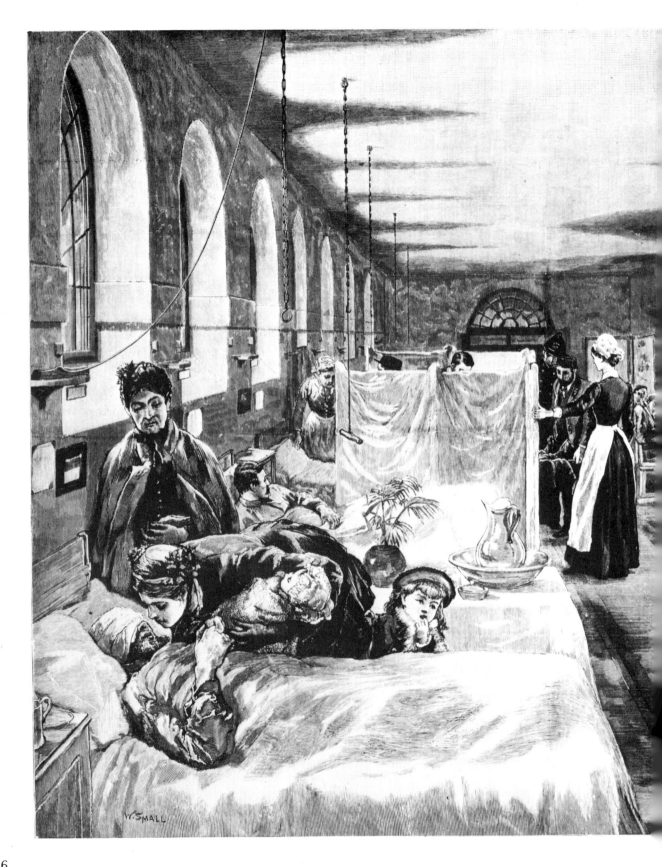

W. SMALL

ing cesspits were found beneath the walls of Windsor Castle. As late as 1871 the Prince of Wales, whose father died of typhoid fever, was infected with the same disease while staying at Londesborough Lodge whose foul drains were responsible for the death of Lord Chesterfield.

Walking through streets littered with dung and excrement, beside rivers from which an almost tangible miasma of decay hovered over the water, breathing air thick with soot, smoke and the smell of putrefying matter, drinking impure water and eating contaminated food, the poor of the large towns not only suffered constantly from a variety of minor complaints but were also repeatedly endangered by epidemics of dangerous diseases. In 1871 23,000 people died of smallpox; and although cholera was rare after the epidemic of 1867, diphtheria, scarlet fever as well as typhoid all continued to claim numerous victims every year. Hundreds of thousands of workers were also exposed to the dangers of industrial diseases. Not only were miners and quarrymen liable to contract diseases of the lungs by the inhalation of toxic dusts; not only were match-tippers prone to necrosis, there were several smaller industries in which workers were exposed to various forms of poisoning, as for instance, the file-cutters of Sheffield who ate their meals in workshops where the atmosphere was impregnated with fine lead-dust.

In cases requiring hospital treatment, the victims viewed the prospect of entering a public ward with the utmost trepidation. For hospitals were extremely uncomfortable institutions, and the risk of cross-infection was acute. 'The very first requirement of a hospital,' wrote Florence Nightingale in 1863, 'is that it should do the sick no harm.' Unfortunately few hospitals met this requirement; and it was often as difficult to get into those that did as to survive treatment in those that did not. In 1859 the rules of Salop Infirmary provided 'that no woman big with child, no child under seven years of age . . . no persons disordered in their senses, suspected to have smallpox or other infectious distemper, having habitual ulcers, cancers not admitting to operation, epileptic or convulsive fits, consumptions, or dropsied in their last illness, in a dying condition, or judged incurable, be admitted as patients, or, inadvertently admitted, be suffered to continue.'

Those who were denied admission to hospital frequently had cause to consider themselves fortunate. For even in the 1890s there were a distressing number of institutions like the workhouse in which the editor of the *British Medical Journal* found the sick 'lying on plank beds with chaff mattresses about three inches thick between their weary bodies and the hard uneven planks . . . Some idiots and imbeciles share the wards with these patients. The infants occupy a dark stone-paved room, bare of furniture, with no rug for the babies to crawl or lie upon and no responsible persons to see to their feeding and cleanliness.'

Places like this were, however, gradually being reformed or replaced. And the use of anaesthetics – which more than one Victorian considered the most valuable of all the inventions of his time – was making the anticipation of surgery less disturbing. Chloroform was first administered as an anaesthetic in 1847 by Sir James Simpson, who had already used ether to relieve the pains of childbirth; and after 1884, when it was discovered that cocaine produced insensitivity to pain if applied to the eye, local anaesthesia was quickly developed. Antiseptic surgery with a carbolic spray was introduced in 1865 by Joseph Lister, and was soon followed by the sterilisation of surgical instruments.

By then Florence Nightingale had started her influential nurses' school at St Thomas' Hospital which was entirely rebuilt in accordance with her insistence on the importance of the free circulation of air and the isolation of patients from each other. At a cost of over £330,000 the architect Henry Currey provided beds for 588 patients in seven detached blocks overlooking the Thames opposite the Palace of Westminster. 'Every ward on each floor has two hydraulic lifts,' *The Illustrated London News* reported when providing its readers with a large drawing of the completed building which was opened by the Queen in 1871: 'one small lift for food or medicines, one larger for taking up patients or nurses. Every ward too has its own bathrooms, lavatories and closets detached from others and its separate shoots for sending down dust and ashes . . . dressings and other things. Natural ventilation is as much as possible depended on, with very simple auxiliary arrangements for cold nights . . . All the building is fireproof . . . The walls of each ward are coated with Parian cement which, while not as cold, is almost as hard and non-absorbent, and quite as smooth, as marble.'

During the next forty years numerous other hospitals were built on these sensible lines all over the country; while others were extended, modernised and, for the most part, administered in a manner which, however haphazard the methods might seem by the standards of today, were nevertheless unrivalled in any other country in Europe.

Indeed, although there was much yet to be done, many reforms to be undertaken and many injustices still to be overcome, the last Victorians could look back with pride on the improvements in society that had been wrought in the sixty years since the Queen had been crowned. As slums were cleared and modern institutions founded, as new housing projects got under way, and as men were more and more aware that the lives of the poor could no longer be disregarded, there dawned the beginning of hope for those still condemned to walk the 'cold, wet, shelterless, midnight streets'.

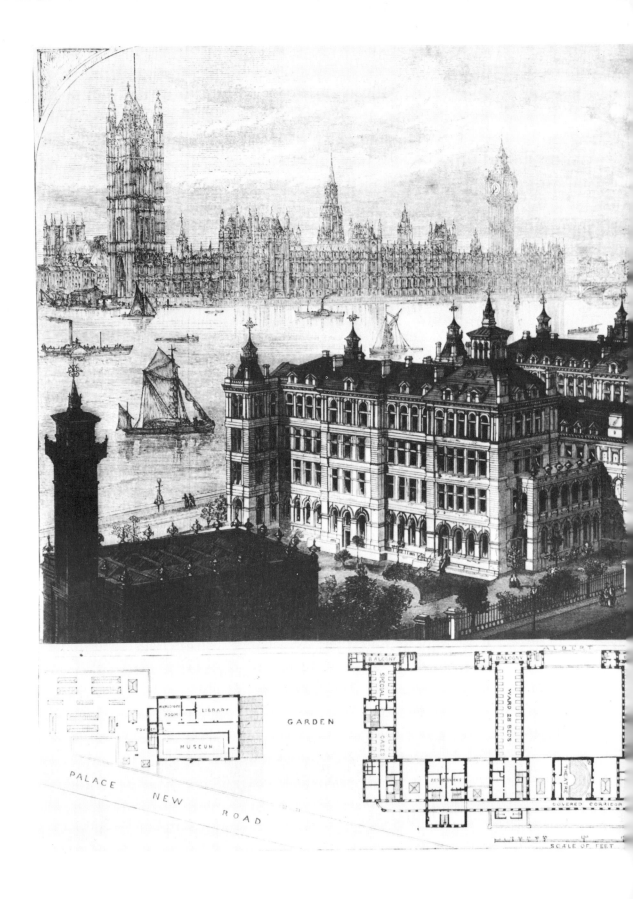

GARDEN

MICROSCOPY
ROOM   LIBRARY

TOWER

MUSEUM

PALACE   NEW   ROAD

ALBERT

BALCONY   BALCONY

SPECIAL CASES

YARD 28 BEDS

RESIDENCES

THEATRE

COVERED CORRIDOR

SCALE OF FEET

T. SULMAN del

PLAN OF ONE PAIR STORY

EMBANKMENT

BALCONY

BALCONY

BALCONY

WARD 28 BEDS

WARD 32 BEDS

WARD 28 BEDS

ROOMS

CHAPEL

THEATRE

ROOMS
FOR
NIGHT
NURSES

COVERED CORRIDOR

RESIDENT
OFFICERS

MEDICAL
ROOMS

ENTRANCE

WESTMINSTER BRIDGE

Epilogue

It was a 'never-to-be-forgotten day', wrote the Queen of her Golden Jubilee when, in celebration of the fiftieth year of her reign, she drove in an open landau through streets thronged with enormous cheering crowds from Paddington Station to Buckingham Palace. It was a day, she thought, which would leave 'heart-stirring memories' behind it for ever. It had been all the more gratifying as she had never expected such enthusiasm: it was not much more than a year before that a hundred guests at a Parliamentary dinner had refused to stand up for the royal toast; that *The Times* had complained that, so rarely did she emerge from the seclusion into which she had retreated since Prince Albert's death, a whole generation had grown up which did not know her.

Encouraged by the reception which the people had given her, she now emerged from that seclusion; and ten years later, on the occasion of her Diamond Jubilee, the 'passionate demonstrations' of loyalty were even more heart-warming. 'No one ever I believe has met with such an ovation as was given to me passing through these six miles of streets,' the Queen confided to her journal. 'The crowds were quite indescribable and their enthusiasm truly marvellous and deeply touching and every face seemed to be filled with real joy.'

Unlike the previous Jubilee her guests were not kings and princes but representatives of that vast colonial Empire which so many thousands of her subjects had been trained to rule, which was the next year to be marked in red upon a postage stamp showing a map of the world above the legend: 'We hold a vaster Empire than has ever been.' And it was this new pride in the Empire which fired the imagination of all classes as they watched the little dumpy figure, still in mourning and shaded from the sun by a parasol of black Chantilly lace, pass through crowded streets on whose decorations a quarter of a million pounds had been spent. As one spectator afterwards observed, expressing a universal sentiment, it was wonderful to think that this small, frail woman riding along with tears of happiness in her eyes, this symbol of the country's prestige, was Empress of India as well as Queen of England, sovereign of an Empire on which the sun never set. 'And you begin to understand as never before what the Empire amounts to,' a journalist wrote, recalling his emotions as the Imperial troops marched past. 'We send out a boy here and a boy there and the boy takes hold of the savages . . . and teaches them to march and shoot . . . and believe in him and die for him and the Queen. A plain, stupid, uninspired people they call us, and yet we are doing this with every kind of savage man there is.'

Opposite Queen Victoria in her landau arriving at the steps of St Paul's Cathedral on the day of her Diamond Jubilee

THE ILLUSTRATED
LONDON NEWS

REGISTERED AT THE GENERAL POST OFFICE AS A NEWSPAPER.

No. 3037.— VOL. CXI.   SATURDAY, JULY 3, 1897.   With Sixteen-Page Supplement } ONE SHILLING.
                                                          and Double-Page Supplement } By Post, 1s. 6½d.

THE ILLUSTRATED
LONDON NEWS.

REGISTERED AT THE GENERAL POST OFFICE AS A NEWSPAPER.

No. 3036.—VOL. CX.   SATURDAY, JUNE 26, 1897.   WITH SIXTEEN-PAGE SUPPLEMENT | ONE SHILLING. By Post, 1s 0 d.

Opposite All the nations of the British Empire uniting to acclaim Victoria after her sixty years as Queen: from the Diamond Jubilee edition of *The Illustrated London News*

Right The Mansion House illuminated to celebrate the Queen's Jubilee: above the pediment shone the Star of India

Below In 1899, the second Boer War broke out in South Africa, and the triumphs of the Diamond Jubilee were quickly forgotten in the military disasters that followed. In this illustration, the City Imperial Volunteers are shown marching off to the war

DOUBLE NUMBER

OF THE

Illustrated London News

DEATH OF THE QUEEN

PRICE ONE SHILLING, BY INLAND POST, 1/0½.

OFFICE, 198, STRAND, LONDON, W.C.

Opposite The end of an era: the death of Queen Victoria on 22 January 1901 was featured by *The London Illustrated News* in a special issue

But this self-congratulatory pride, this confidence, this mood of what had recently become known as jingoism did not long remain unclouded. Two years after the Diamond Jubilee, the Boer War broke out as the result of a raid by Dr Jameson, Administrator of Rhodesia, who had led a force of mounted policemen into the Transvaal to raise a rebellion against President Kruger. And this war – the first against a white enemy which the Victorian army had fought since the Crimean War of 1854–6 – revealed at once how slender were British claims to military supremacy and how deeply Britain's pretensions were resented by the rest of the world.

Before the century was over men began to question the reality of that order and stability, that power and confidence which had seemed so characteristically Victorian. And the death of the Queen in the first year of the new century was recognised, even at the time, as marking the end of an era. On that February morning when her coffin, mounted on a gun carriage and with the Royal Standard thrown partially over the pall, was transported to Windsor, people could be seen weeping in the purple-draped streets and in the fields where they had knelt to watch the royal train go by. 'Lamenting the passing of a way of life,' as one of the mourners put it, 'they looked with apprehension to an uncertain future.' It was as though the Queen alone had been supposed capable of holding back the unwelcome changes that were to come.

Yet the Victorian age itself had been one of profound political, economic and social reform. There was no class whose way of life had not been transformed. These great changes, as a writer in *The Illustrated London News* observed, were 'not all for the better. But the age which this journal has witnessed has been an age which, if its faults have been many, men will remember with wonder, gratitude and respect.'

Selected Bibliography

These are some of the principal works consulted in addition to the files of *The Illustrated London News:*

ABEL-SMITH, Brian, *The Hospitals* (1964)

ALTICK, Richard D., *Victorian People and Ideas* (1973)

BEST, Geoffrey, *Mid-Victorian Britain 1851–75* (1971)

BLACK, Eugene C. (Ed.), *Victorian Culture and Society* (1973)

BOOTH, Charles, *Charles Booth's London* (Ed. Albert Fried and Richard Elman, 1969)

BRIGGS, Asa, *Victorian Cities* (1963)

BURNETT, John, *Useful Toil* (1974)

BURTON, Elizabeth, *The Early Victorians at Home* (1972)

CHATHAM, J. H., *An Economic History of Modern Britain* (1926)

CHESNEY, Kellow, *The Victorian Underworld* (1970)

CLARK, G. Kitson, *The Making of Victorian England* (1962)

DYOS, H. J. and Michael WOLFF (Eds), *The Victorian City. Images and Realities* (1973)

ENSOR, R. C. K., *England, 1870–1914* (1964)

GIROUARD, Mark, *The Victorian Country House* (1971)

HARRISON, J. F. C., *The Early Victorians, 1832–1851* (1971)

HIBBERT, Christopher, *The Roots of Evil* (1963)

MAYHEW, Henry, *London Labour and the London Poor* (Ed. Peter Quennell, 1950–1)

LOCHHEAD, Marion, *The Victorian Household* (1964)

MITCHELL, R. J. and M. D. R. LEYS, *A History of the English People* (1950)

PERKIN, Harold, *The Origins of Modern English Society* (1969)

READER, W. J., *Victorian England* (1964)

WOODWARD, Sir Llewellyn, *The Age of Reform, 1815–1870* (1962)

YOUNG, G. M. (Ed.), *Early Victorian England* (1934)